WHY TRIDENT?

Commander Robert Forsyth RN (Ret'd)

SPOKESMAN

First published in 2020

Spokesman
5 Churchill Park
Nottingham, NG4 2HF, England
www.spokesmanbooks.com

Spokesman is the publishing imprint of the Bertrand Russell Peace Foundation Ltd.

ISBN 978 085124 8905

A cataloguing-in-publication (CIP) record is available from the British Library.

Cover photo: downloaded from defenceimagery.mod.uk and used under the MOD
(Consent Licence) and OGL (Open Government Licence).

Contents

Appendices

Foreword

Vice Admiral Sir Jeremy Blackham KCB MA

The British submarine-borne nuclear deterrent was first deployed in 1969, at the height of the Cold War, and has been an unchallengeable cornerstone of British defence and security ever since. But in that time much has changed. Many more countries now possess, or have the means to possess, nuclear weapons; international relationships are different and more complex; critical threats emanate from non-state actors. British international influence has declined, not least because of her reduced conventional military power and the growth of new forms of warfare, perhaps less amenable to nuclear dissuasion. However, the conventional forces that Britain has chosen to retain are now sufficiently reduced to lower very significantly the nuclear threshold, the point at which a decision to use nuclear weapons or rather to seek an accommodation is reached. Some people, of whom I am one, believe that a lower nuclear threshold greatly undermines the credibility of our nuclear deterrent because an adversary with far greater conventional and nuclear capability may not believe we would use it, or may conclude that he can win a conventional war before he has exhausted his conventional options or before we have found ourselves at a level of threat which could justify unleashing mutual nuclear destruction. Deterrence would have failed before nuclear forces came into play. One might even argue that we have deterred ourselves rather than the enemy.

Deterrence is an intellectually challenging subject and one in which no nation can afford to act without careful consideration of the interests of its allies and even those of its potential rivals. In the interconnected world in which we live, and the many natural and technological challenges, as well as the more conventional military threats we face, it is impossible to over-emphasise the value of being able to deter at any level of warfare, to prevent us reaching the nuclear threshold. Against this background, the United Kingdom has declared its intention to carry out a fundamental defence and security review, with the aim of reshaping its defence and security posture to meet the new challenges and those of the next generation. This is crucially important in an increasingly dangerous world.

Such a review must be a "clean sheet" review; nothing should be sacrosanct. It must produce a policy which is coherent "end-to-end" and equipped with the best and most effective tools we are prepared to afford. It is therefore very timely to review the nuclear element of our deterrent posture, in the light of the moral, legal, economic, political, environmental and practical issues involved. We can no longer simply assume that it is in all circumstances essential, irrespective of its impact on our overall security. Few people have examined more rigorously the critical questions surrounding the nuclear element of this "continuum of deterrence" than Rob Forsyth. I am very glad that his work in this field has been collected into this book. All those involved in this field should read and carefully reflect on what he has to say.

Vice Admiral Blackham served as Deputy Commander-in-Chief, Fleet and, in retirement, was Editor of The Naval Review.

Introduction

Professor Nick Grief BA PhD Barrister

It is a great pleasure to have been invited to introduce this excellent compilation of articles. I first met Commander Rob Forsyth at Doughty Street Chambers, London, in September 2018. A group of us were discussing strategies for challenging the UK Government's deployment of *Trident*. Having become convinced about the illegality of nuclear weapons as a young academic in the early 1980s when the United Kingdom was deploying *Polaris*, *Trident's* predecessor, at sea, I was intrigued to meet this former Executive Officer of a *Polaris* submarine ("the other half of the two-man launch authorisation team") who now, as he puts it, falls "firmly in the nuclear deterrence doubters' bracket".

It has been fascinating to hear Rob talk about his experiences of submarine life and explain the missile firing protocol of his day, and to listen to his concerns about the military's apparent lack of involvement today in any decision to launch *Trident*. I have also had the privilege of commenting on Rob's three articles in Chapter II and on his submission to Parliament's Public Administration and Constitutional Affairs Committee in Chapter III.

What comes through these personal reflections is Rob's dogged determination to get at the truth about nuclear deterrence, to expose the policy's shortcomings and, despite "lengthy but ultimately frustrating correspondence with the MoD" which only strengthened his "resolve to probe deeper", to go on asking questions about the legal and moral implications of the Government's position for today's SSBN Commanding Officers who "in very different circumstances to my day, have a much greater problem in how they respond to an order to fire".

Because of Rob's admission that he and his captain would not have been prepared to launch *Polaris* as a First Strike, it has been alleged that he violated the principle that military leaders do not subvert their democratic political leadership. This is a very serious allegation and in my view wholly unfounded, especially as Rob is quite clear that First Strike was not an option they were briefed about. It begs the question: how do we define patriotism? Does love for one's country mean, as Cecil Spring-Rice proposed: "The love that asks no question"? Or is not a better view, as Keith W Clements argued in *A Patriotism for Today* (published in 1984 but still highly relevant), that: "We do have to ask questions about the morality of the national cause for which the sacrifice is made, otherwise devotion becomes indistinguishable from fanaticism"?

Readers will find much to challenge their thinking on the issues broached here. Thanks to the wisdom and generosity of the Bertrand Russell Peace Foundation, this compelling and timely collection will have the wider readership it clearly deserves.

Professor Nick Grief is Emeritus Professor of Law at the University of Kent and an Associate Tenant at Doughty Street Chambers. He was closely involved in the World Court Project which led to the International Court of Justice's Advisory Opinion on 'the Legality of the Threat or Use of Nuclear Weapons' in July 1996.

CHAPTER I

The case against UK Trident
A Naval Officer's Perspective
First published in *Warship International Fleet Review, July 2018*

This article was published in *Warship International Fleet Review* (*WIFR*) in July 2018. It was specially adapted from a talk given by Cdr Forsyth to a conference hosted by the National Museum of The Royal Navy on 15 June 2018 entitled *Silent & Secret* marking the 50th anniversary of the start of the RN's Polaris patrols. The Conference was attended by RN, MoD and a number of NGO's involved in the defence sector.

WIFR Editor's Introduction
Commander Rob Forsyth was Executive Officer (XO) of the *Polaris* missile submarine *HMS Repulse* in the early mid-1970s and, as such, performed as one of the front line custodians of the UK's nuclear deterrent at the height of the Cold War confrontation between Russia and the West. In this commentary he questions the relevance of this nation maintaining a Continuous at Sea Deterrent in an era when it seems barely able to field conventional military forces. He suggests a more sensible option might be to discard *Trident* altogether.

* * *

In common with a number of my peers, I have in recent times grown increasingly concerned about the state into which the Royal Navy has declined.

It now seems to be so small that it will be unable to offer much more than an escort group for one of the new strike carriers. This will severely affect its ability to conduct Anti-Submarine Warfare (ASW) and other operations at a time when Russian activity is returning to Cold War levels. There are also numerous other demands on its people and units, not least in the waters of Arabia, Asia-Pacific and around UK sovereign territories scattered across the globe.

The RN's decline has unquestionably been caused by successive cuts in public spending. Yet it is noticeable that there is one part of the defence budget that is not only protected but continues to grow – the proportion devoted to the Continuous at Sea Deterrent (CASD). The UK's conventional war-fighting capability is being sacrificed to preserve its nuclear one. Some £2 billion a year is needed to maintain CASD and the cost of the four new *Dreadnought* Class ballistic submarines (SSBNs) will likely exceed £40 billion.

For the same money the UK could have had at least another eight attack submarines (SSNs) or – better still – a mix of conventional and nuclear boats and 15 (or more) extra frigates.

However, the issues at stake stretch beyond the numbers game and also include the worrying state of the UK Government's strategic nuclear defence policy.

Some serious questions need to be asked (and answered) by the national political and military leadership about not only the affordability of CASD, but also its necessity at all and/or – if it is retained – the moral context of its use. It is often said that the UK retains its nuclear weapons to remain one of the five nuclear weapon power players – colloquially known as the P5 – and to retain the UK's seat at the United Nations Security Council (UNSC). The reality is that, as a signatory to the 1968 Nuclear Non-Proliferation Treaty, each of the 'P5s' retains their seat even if they give up nuclear weapons.

Also, just whom is the UK trying to deter? Where is the massive state based strategic threat to Europe today that replicates the Cold War Soviets? Where is the nuclear-armed rogue state with direct hostile military intent towards the UK? Neither Iran, North Korea nor Syria currently have military designs on the UK and no one in their right mind would consider *Trident* an appropriate weapon to use against terrorist organisations such as ISIL. The logic of spending £2 billion a year to sustain *Trident* on CASD duties 'just in case' therefore has to be questioned, especially when the patrolling submarine's missiles are not targeted, nor are they even held at 15 minutes to fire. It also uses scarce ships, submarines and air assets to sustain its invulnerability.

Also, is it really independent? When we purchased and managed our own *Polaris* missiles, the UK could make some claim to possessing an independent deterrent in that the weapons could be deployed and fired under total UK control; albeit we were heavily dependent in the long run on US support for supply of spares (and also for missile testing and satellite guidance facilities).

Today the UK uses the shared *Trident* missile facility at Kings Bay, Georgia and is even more heavily dependent on the USA. The Americans could deny us access to their stock of missiles if it suited them. The British American Security Information Council (BASIC) report to Parliament in 2014 pointed out: "If the US were to withdraw their cooperation completely the UK nuclear capability would probably have a life expectancy measured in months".

The UK remains closely integrated with the US Navy's nuclear propulsion and weapon programmes – even to the point of the Royal Navy and US Navy today designing a common submarine missile module for their respective next generation ballistic missile submarines (SSBNs). I cannot conceive Britain would ever fire its *Trident* missiles without the Americans' political support and, if they so wished, I am fully confident they would find a way to frustrate the UK. The Government assertion that the UK operates an independent deterrent is no more than national hubris.

The next item of intellectual 'emperor's new clothes' frequently worn by avid supporters of maintaining and replacing the UK's CASD is the contention that 'you cannot un-invent nuclear weapons'. Neither can you uninvent chemical weapons of course, but they are internationally outlawed as unacceptable Weapons of Mass Destruction (WMD). That is why the USA, UK and France attacked Syrian chemical warfare facilities in April 2018. Chemical and biological weapons are so stigmatised that there is no thought of using them as a deterrence. Ironically, nuclear weapons, which are orders of magnitude more destructive, lethal and longer lasting in their poisoning effects, are also called WMD but are not banned. Where is the logic in that?

But war is an ugly business, some would say, to which rules do not apply. The legendary WWII submarine captain Alastair Mars, on patrol in the Java Sea in his boat *HMS Thule* in 1945, would have disagreed. For example, on the occasion that he had an enemy hospital ship in his sights – an easy kill after many frustrating weeks trying to sink warship targets – he simply lowered *Thule's* periscope. He later wrote of this moment that he made the decision not to attack because "if a man is to remain civilised he must have rules".

As a former captain of both a diesel-electric patrol submarine and nuclear-powered hunter-killer, and a one-time teacher of the perisher course, I found what Mars wrote a good example of fine moral judgement in a situation where temptation may have been great. To that end, in the process of investigating the current state of affairs with regard to the UK's nuclear deterrent force, I took a close look at how national nuclear policy conforms to International Humanitarian Law.

The Nuremberg Charter and Geneva Conventions have long governed the conduct of war and, before the first of my four *Polaris* patrols, my Commanding Officer and I formally discussed whether we were totally in agreement that an order to fire our missiles as a SECOND strike was lawful – i.e. enacting the policy of Mutually Assured Destruction (MAD).

We agreed it was, but we added that, if there was no other indication that a nuclear attack by the foe was under way, we would pause the countdown, discuss and even possibly phone home (so to speak). Since 2002 the UK has followed a policy of sub-strategic, so-called Flexible Response, that entails potentially using a single warhead – this being still eight times the power of the Hiroshima bomb – on each *Trident* missile. The UK has also reduced the number of missiles/warheads embarked in an SSBN.

This at least shows willingness by the UK to take the lead in reducing weapons stocks; but not all is as it seems. Various statements have made it clear that the policy is now one of deliberate ambiguity as to when and how the UK's nuclear missiles would be used. For example:

- "[The] UK is prepared to use nuclear weapons against rogue states such as Iraq if they ever used weapons of mass destruction against British troops in the field." Defence Secretary's statement to MPs, March 20, 2002
- "the Government will not rule in or out the first use of nuclear weapons." Government White Paper, May 8, 2015

That represents a significant shift away from the certainty of last resort/second strike of my days at sea. It also seems to ignore the fact that the Geneva Conventions and the more recent International Criminal Court Statute (2002) of Rome – which refers to their use as a 'war crime' – do not countenance the use of any form of WMD and certainly not in first use. I was therefore concerned as to how the Prime Minister could provide certainty to SSBN Commanding Officers that they would not be called upon to carry out what might be viewed as a war crime. A CO has a personal responsibility under Military Law to assure himself he is not obeying an illegal order. This is a matter a number of US senior officers have publicly addressed, stating that they may not obey an order to fire if they think it might not be legal.

So, in 2017, I wrote to the UK Ministry of Defence (MoD) Nuclear Policy department and asked them the legal position for British SSBN captains. I received a response in writing that stated, among other things: "Our nuclear Deterrent is fully compliant and compatible with our international treaty and legal obligations". More surprising were actions the UK Government has taken to enable the MoD to say that [see Chapter IV].

In 1977 the UK signed a new Protocol attached to the Geneva Conventions. It contained stringent provisions for the protection of civilians from the use of WMD. In 1998 the Government attached a Reservation to this Protocol which stated "the rules ...do not have any effect on and do not regulate or prohibit the use of Nuclear Weapons". They repeated this Reservation again in 2002.

So, while on the one hand the UK was actively negotiating international agreements outlawing chemical and biological weapons, on the other hand it was absolving itself from any restriction on using nuclear ones. I wonder just how many people know about this?

Certainly the vast majority of the general public are probably unaware of it and I wonder if SSBN Commanding Officers are too?

As further support for legality, in its response to me the MoD selectively quoted the 1996 International Court of Justice's Advisory Opinion on a question from the UN General Assembly (as to whether the threat or use of nuclear weapons complied with international humanitarian law). The MoD suggested it "was not necessarily unlawful in extreme circumstance".

In fact, the 14 Judges that sit on the Court were evenly divided in their opinion as to whether, in the very extreme circumstance of the existence of a state being threatened, their use in self-defence – i.e. second use – might be justified. France, the USA and UK voted for it being lawful but, interestingly, Russia and China voted it unlawful.

The President of the court made a separate Declaration that this vote should not be interpreted as leaving the door open to an interpretation that their use *was* lawful.

Also, what the MoD did not mention to me was that all 14 Judges had, in a previous opinion, unanimously confirmed that "the threat or use of nuclear weapons should be compatible with the requirements of international law applicable in armed conflict" e.g. The Geneva Conventions.

On the face of it this means that the threat of second use, never mind first, would always require considerable debate and legal consideration beforehand.

In its response to me the MoD also said that legality could, in the end, only be decided on a case-by-case basis. This further underscored my concern for the position of SSBN captains – the MoD seems to be trying to ensure the buck stops with the submarine captain, who may well be the person least qualified to decide that firing nuclear missiles is appropriate. In 2017 the UK Government took a further step away from being accountable for its own nuclear policy by revising the declaration, which accepts the compulsory jurisdiction of the International Court of Justice. According to BASIC "the revised Declaration also includes a reservation excluding from the Court's jurisdiction any cases related to Nuclear Weapons and/or nuclear disarmament unless the other four Nuclear Non-Proliferation Treaty (NPT) nuclear-weapons States also accept the Court's jurisdiction with respect to the case". The chances of all P5 states agreeing to accept jurisdiction simultaneously is, of course, just about zero.

The UK holds itself up as a protector of international standards – even to the extent of going to war in Iraq and supporting strikes on Syrian chemical weapon sites. The then Prime Minister, Theresa May, in justifying the bombardment of Syria in Parliament on April 16 2018, echoed Alastair Mars when she said, "we need to stand up for the global rules and standards that keep us safe".

Should not the standards that legislate against us (or anyone else) using chemical and biological WMD also apply against us (or anyone else) using nuclear WMD?

The rest of the non-nuclear weapons world certainly thinks this should be the case. One hundred and twenty-two nations, fed up with the lack of action by the P5, put in place a Treaty on the Prohibition of Nuclear Weapons in 2017. The UK chose not to be associated with this in any way, nor did the UK send a senior government representative to the Nobel Peace Prize ceremony to honour the *International Campaign to Abolish Nuclear Weapons* group who were largely responsible for achieving the Treaty. SSBN operators France and the USA also only sent junior officials, though Russia and China did send senior representatives.

It's worth noting that in its letter to me, of April 12 2018 [see page 66], the MoD stated: "We consider the step by step approach to multilateral nuclear disarmament delivered through the Nuclear Non-Proliferation Treaty (signed 1968) as the cornerstone of efforts to pursue the goal".

Actually, the UK has not actively participated in or encouraged multilateral disarmament negotiations since the Comprehensive Nuclear Test Ban Treaty in 1996 – 24 years ago. Why does the UK ignore treaty obligations, reject International Humanitarian Law, and follow a policy of ambiguity as to when and in what circumstances it might use nuclear weapons? Could it be because the weakness of UK conventional forces is recognised and possessing the nuclear deterrent force is seen to be a counter-balance to such inferiority? Why else would the UK Government take all these actions – or not take in the case of multilateral negotiations – all while simultaneously insisting that other countries observe the ban on the lesser evil of chemical and biological weapons?

I think the UK should immediately do the following:

• Say NO to First Use under any circumstances.
• Revoke the Reservation regarding use of nuclear weapons placed on Protocol 1 to The Geneva Conventions.
• Recognise the authority of the International Court of Justice on all matters relating to the use of nuclear weapons.

These actions would re-establish the moral standing of the UK in world affairs and, in so doing, resolve the problem for today's SSBN captains whom, I believe, could otherwise be placed in legal jeopardy. In addition we can stand down from CASD.

There is no threat that justifies such an aggressive posture at present. The immediate cost benefit would be only three boats required to maintain the operational capability and still be capable of reverting to CASD if an existential threat appears.

Taking the argument in an even more radical direction, as there is no credible strategic threat to our nation – and the UK cannot afford CASD anyway and would not actually lose its seat on the UNSC – it should offer to cancel the *Dreadnought* submarine programme as a significant bargaining tool in multilateral negotiations.

For it is now clear that the 1968 Nuclear Non-Proliferation Treaty, far from limiting the spread of nuclear weapons is actually having the reverse effect – they are proliferating at an alarming rate in the hands of states not signed up to the NPT. There must be a major global multilateral disarmament initiative. UK support for the Treaty on the Prohibition of Nuclear Weapons would be a good start to the process. This would also demonstrate to the rest of the world that UK is taking multilateral disarmament seriously – for the first time in more than two decades.

Once the decision has been taken to denuclearise the UK then scarce surface warship, submarine and air assets could be usefully deployed elsewhere. There would be the funds to construct UK Armed Forces of sufficient size and capability to play a key role in conventional deterrence in NATO.

In 2016, during the Commons debate on replacing the current *Trident* submarines, Prime Minister Theresa May claimed that Parliamentary opponents of the UK's nuclear deterrent were "first to defend the country's enemies". I would suggest that is far from being the case. This patriot – who has served at the coal face of the at-sea deterrent – is merely asking the UK's leaders to start thinking hard about the nation's strategic choices and introduce some bold moves. The UK would be showing true global leadership at a time when the whole of humanity could so easily topple over the edge into a nuclear annihilation abyss.

Revised for publication in this volume, October 2020.

CHAPTER II

UK nuclear deterrence policy and the Trident nuclear weapon system

First published on www.whytrident.uk, May 2020

Part 1 – The Concept of Nuclear Deterrence*

This first part of a series of three articles summarises why I undertook to research a concept I once took for granted and the results of that research; Part 2 reviews current UK nuclear weapon policy; Part 3 examines international and military law on the threat or use of nuclear weapons, the UK Government's position, and how it affects Trident submarine Commanding Officers.

My experience

In 1962, months into being appointed to my first submarine, *HMS Auriga*, we sailed on war patrol in response to the Cuban missile crisis as part of a US-led naval blockade tasked with detecting Soviet submarines south of the Iceland-Faroes gap. I therefore was a Cold War warrior from the start, fully convinced of the Soviet threat and the need to counter it. Following command of *HMS Alliance* (1970-72), I was appointed Executive Officer of the Starboard Crew of the *Polaris* nuclear-armed ballistic missile submarine (SSBN) *HMS Repulse*. Before our first patrol, my Commanding Officer (CO) and I discussed the procedures for receipt of an order to fire and whether we were both fully committed to obeying it. As his second in command I was

---

the other half of the two-man launch authorisation team, so we needed to be clear with each other. He told me that we would only be ordered to fire if the Soviets fired nuclear missiles at the UK or our NATO allies first. We agreed that, under those circumstances, we would retaliate; but the chances of being called upon to do so were small, because both East and West recognised that what would ensue would be 'Mutually Assured Destruction' (MAD). Nonetheless, our response might have limited further nuclear exchanges.

At that time international law was silent on the specific use of nuclear weapons, but the Geneva Conventions implied their use would be unlawful because their massive and indiscriminate effects would inevitably kill millions of civilians. However, we did not know what our targets were, because targeting was by means of coded tapes; but we did know that military installations were located in or near heavily populated cities. We wryly called this deliberate policy the 'Aunt in Minsk syndrome' – that if we knew we had an aunt there, we might refrain from firing. We also agreed that if a simple check of the BBC News showed no sign of the UK being under attack and programmes were transmitting as usual, then we would not fire but pause and, against all the rules, 'phone home' to question the firing order.

I carried out four patrols in *HMS Repulse*, before being appointed Commanding Officer ('Teacher') of the submarine CO's Qualifying Course (dubbed for good reasons the 'Perisher') followed by command of *HMS Sceptre*, a new build SSN. Some desk time followed in the Ministry of Defence (MoD) (Operational Requirements), whereupon I took voluntary retirement in 1981, and subsequently spent some 25 years in a career in industry, experiencing a somewhat wider perspective on the world.

My growing concern

In 2015, in final retirement, I began to take a serious interest in the declining state of the Navy. Over the next few years, I carried out an in-depth examination of the rationale for, and cost of, the UK *Trident* programme. This led me into researching the history of UK nuclear weapon policy and the evolution of international humanitarian law. My experience of command and my time as 'Teacher', coupled with a view of the world now de-coupled from accepted naval thinking, led to a growing awareness that today's *Trident* SSBN COs, in very different circumstances to my day, have a much greater problem in how they respond to an order to fire.

A new *Polaris* warhead, code-named *Chevaline*, was introduced into service as I was leaving the Navy. The justification for this very secret and costly programme was that, to sustain the credibility of the UK's nuclear deterrence policy, the RN *Polaris* force needed the capability to take out military command and control installations in Moscow[1], which were protected by increasingly capable anti-ballistic missile systems. Prior to that, US and UK *Polaris* had mainly been targeted at cities and therefore at millions of 'Aunts in Minsk'.

I observed the completed replacement of *Polaris* by *Trident* in 1996 with interest; but I wondered what would happen to this over-capable, hugely expensive programme as the Soviet threat receded with the end of the Cold War. US, UK and Russian nuclear arsenals were reduced; deployed strategic systems mutually de-targeted; and in 1998 the new Labour Government unilaterally relaxed the alert state of *Trident* to several days.[2] I presumed that it would be stood down from Continuous At Sea Deterrence (CASD) but remain operationally available as insurance. I also thought our deterrent policy remained one of second strike, because of repeated Government assurances that the UK would only use *Trident* as a weapon of 'last resort.' The commitment to disarmament contained in Article VI of the 1968 Nuclear Non-Proliferation Treaty (NPT)[3] seemed to be no longer utopian.

Of greater concern to many ex-service people was the steady decline in our conventional forces as successive UK Governments took the opportunity to cut the Defence budget. This alarming trend accelerated under the fiscal austerity policies adopted following the 2008 worldwide financial crisis. The Fleet's capabilities have now been reduced to the point where the essential escalating stepping-stones of conventional deterrence before a threshold of nuclear use is reached have been dangerously removed, such that the UK's nuclear deterrence posture is no longer credible.

In 2016, during the debate in Parliament to replace the four *Vanguard* class submarines with the *Dreadnought* class and a new nuclear warhead programme, I began to question the fast escalating costs – both financial and in terms of operational strain on the RN – of maintaining CASD against a future unknown threat. Delays in the *Dreadnought* programme now entailed running on the obsolete *Vanguard* class for 6-8 years longer than the *Resolution* class. I wondered whether these costs were justified in light of the severe reduction in the UK's conventional ability to defend against the diverse, newly emerging threats. The worsening relations between NATO and Russia threatening re-expansion back into former Soviet satellite states are of a far less extreme order to the Soviet threat of world domination, but will require credible conventional forces to deter any such ambitions.

The arguments put forward owed less to how best to defend the realm, and more to the fact that giving up *Trident* would denude the UK of a prestigious international role. It became apparent to me that all studies prior to the decision to proceed with *Trident* replacement presumed the continuing need for a UK (so-called) 'deterrent'. Any discussion seemed more about how best to deliver this, rather than an objective examination of whether the UK actually needed nuclear deterrence in the first place.

The 2016 debate struck me as an exercise in self-righteous rhetoric, noticeably short on facts, in which *Trident* supporters competed to be patriots and sought to brand any dissenters as traitors. The tone was very much "Never mind the question – the answer is *Trident*". Furthermore, Mrs May's flat "Yes" to the question "Is she personally prepared to authorise a nuclear strike that could kill 100,000 innocent men, women and children?" alarmed me. Just why was the PM – and to be fair, her predecessors – so totally wedded to *Trident* beyond any reasonable discussion? This was also generally accepted by the media and public. They seemed unaware that, come the need to resist a serious threat, it will now be little more than a single step to reach the nuclear option in order to offset a lack of sufficient conventional military force.

Twenty-five years in industry gave me a healthy instinct to always look behind Government statements. Time had also eroded the habit of conformity that military service inevitably induces. To help my research, I conducted a lengthy but ultimately frustrating correspondence with the MoD Nuclear Policy Department.[5] The responses carefully avoided answering my questions, which were directed at finding out how SSBN COs reconciled current international and military law on the use of nuclear weapons with their responsibility to observe them. MoD's unattributed replies – which gave the uneasy impression of having come from the Ministry of Truth in George Orwell's *1984* – repeatedly made unsupported assertions of legal compliance (which I discuss in Part 3). This strengthened my resolve to probe deeper. [see Chapter IV for the full correspondence]

Does nuclear deterrence work?

Forty-odd years on from accepting without question that nuclear deterrence worked, I re-addressed the concept. After considerable research it became clear that there is no proof 'beyond reasonable doubt' that nuclear weapons deter the use of nuclear weapons by others or have prevented any of the major wars that have occurred since 1945.

Sir Michael Quinlan, the arch-proponent of the UK's nuclear deterrence policy, admitted he was only providing "intellectual clothing for a gut decision" by successive UK Governments.[6] Following the Soviet collapse he added ruefully that he had "perhaps been stuck in adversary patterns of thinking". Former PM Tony Blair also confessed in his autobiography to ambivalence: "...[T]he utility in a post-Cold War world is less in terms of deterrence and non-existent in terms of military use... I opted to renew it [*Trident*]. But the contrary decision would not have been stupid."[7] In 2015 George Shultz, US Secretary of State 1982-89, wrote that he now believed nuclear weapons "...were, and are, the gravest threat to humanity's survival. Their effect in preventing wars has been overrated."[8]

Even when the US held a nuclear monopoly it did not stop Stalin interfering in Berlin, or North Korea invading the South supported by China; likewise Ho Chi Minh in Vietnam; Egypt attacking nuclear-armed Israel in 1973; Argentina invading the Falklands in 1982 (threatened use of *Polaris* was not credible); Iraq attacking Kuwait in 1990; and repeated dangerous confrontations between India and Pakistan after they both acquired nuclear weapons in 1998. The latter's '1999 Kargil war' upended nuclear deterrence theory, when Pakistan felt emboldened to send military forces into disputed territory because it mistakenly believed its nuclear capability would deter India, when instead it provoked rapid escalation which was only ended after intervention by US President Clinton.

The 1962 Cuban missile crisis is often cited as an example of where nuclear deterrence worked. But did it? Soviet President Khrushchev was not deterred from deploying nuclear-tipped missiles in the first place, to protect Cuba from US invasion. This was also to counter US *Jupiter* missiles deployed to Turkey and in US submarines patrolling off the Pacific coast of the USSR.[9] We now know that Khrushchev withdrew the Cuba missiles because he became increasingly fearful of his own forces being provoked by US threats into accidentally or irresponsibly using them, and because of US President Kennedy's unpublicised face-saving offer to withdraw the US missiles from Turkey. Khrushchev's fear was justified when Soviet Navy Second Captain Arkhipov refused to authorise the CO of his 'F' class submarine to launch one of its three, 15 kiloton, nuclear-tipped torpedoes at a blockading US escort dropping explosive charges to "encourage" him to surface. This first came to light at a former decision-makers' conference hosted by President Castro in Cuba in 2002.[10]

The other reality is that the use of nuclear weapons by miscalculation, mistake or malfunction, is much the most likely way that a nuclear exchange could be instigated. In 1983 Yuri Andropov, Soviet General Secretary, recognised this when he said: "Nuclear war could occur not through evil intent but could happen through miscalculation".[11] A Chatham House report, *Too Close for Comfort*[12], examines the record of such risks, identifying at least 13 separate occasions when the world came extremely close to accidental nuclear war. An example in 2018 involved a false initiation of a nuclear warning alarm in Hawaii at a time when North Korea was threatening a missile attack against US territory.[13] Sir Rodric Braithwaite, UK Ambassador to the Soviet Union in 1991-92, eloquently summed up the paradox of nuclear deterrence: "…[Y]ou intend to terrify your enemy into behaving properly; but you risk frightening him into doing something silly."[14]

All of this is discussed in considerable depth by many authoritative sources, from which I found four authors of particular value:

Sir Michael Quinlan: *Thinking about Nuclear Weapons: Principles, Problems, Prospects* (Oxford University Press, 2009). Quinlan was the Permanent Under-Secretary of State at the MoD 1988-92 and a leading advocate for nuclear deterrence and proponent of UK nuclear weapon policy.

Sir Rodric Braithwaite: *Armageddon and Paranoia: The Nuclear Confrontation* (Profile Books, 2017) It was illuminating to read in his book that "…There is no evidence that the Russians ever hoped to incorporate Western Europe by military means".[15] Furthermore, he reported that "the British Prime Minister told the Russian President in January 1992 that the British nuclear deterrent consisted of four ballistic missile submarines of which only one was on patrol at any given moment. Boris Yeltsin at first seemed surprised but recovered his composure and indicated generously that he didn't think he needed to worry too much about such a small force".[16]

Mr Daniel Ellsberg: *The Doomsday Machine: Confessions of a Nuclear War Planner* (Bloomsbury USA, 2017). Ellsberg worked as a strategic analyst at the RAND Corporation in the 1950s and 60s concentrating on US nuclear strategy. His account of US policy and (lack of) command and control of nuclear weapons makes for very uncomfortable reading and reaches forward to similar concerns in the US Forces today (to be discussed in Part 3).

Cdr Robert Green RN (Ret'd): *Security without Nuclear Deterrence* (Spokesman Books, 2018). The substantial Foreword to this very well researched book is by Vice Admiral Sir Jeremy Blackham and should be required reading by politicians. He articulates very clearly his concerns about the loss of a graduated UK conventional deterrence capability and concludes that "it is not possible to separate nuclear doctrine, force structure and strength from conventional force structure and strength, across an increasingly wide range of non-nuclear war making capabilities".[17] This will be discussed in more depth in Part 2.

Summary

After several years' study, discussion and thought, I now fall firmly into the nuclear deterrence doubters' bracket. However, I accept that others, just as sincerely, do not – though they recognise the dangers of nuclear capability ownership and fully support multilateral nuclear disarmament. Interestingly, China seems to fall into this category (more on this in Part 2). Those who most concern me avowedly believe in nuclear deterrence, not for the principle but because they believe possession confers indispensable political power. These include the Governments of the five self-appointed 'responsible' recognised nuclear weapon States (generally known as the P5): the US, Russia, China, France and the UK – the latter desperately trying to keep up with the US upon which it depends for its nuclear capability, and refusing to contemplate France as the sole European nuclear power. Of the remaining nuclear-armed states, Israel struggles to maintain ambiguity; conversely, India and Pakistan flaunt their capability. This leaves North Korea, which uniquely uses its development of nuclear weapons not so much to deter attacks on itself as to trade them for international recognition, by exploiting the power of ownership rather than relying on nuclear deterrence for strategic defence.

A combination of false intelligence, lobbying by the military and their equipment suppliers, and political power play has encouraged a nuclear arms race in order to justify the continuance of nuclear deterrence – a vicious circle of self-confirmation. A "gut decision" is leading to expenditure on a weapon system which the UK has not had occasion to target for 24 years and, by admittance, may not ever do so, let alone use it. Moreover, it is denying its military the usable weapon systems which are badly needed to deter existing threats. As Vice Admiral Blackham reiterates in his Foreword to Green's book, "the cardinal point is that the nuclear deterrent is not, and cannot be, a substitute for conventional capabilities. The credibility of flexible response depends upon deferring any decision to use nuclear weapons until the very existence of the nation is at stake. This requirement means that the conventional forces must be of sufficient capability to deal with any lesser threat; and that one's potential enemy must believe this to be so."[18]

Revised for publication in this volume, October 2020.

Part 2 – A Review of UK Nuclear Weapon Policy*

Is *Trident* independent?

The justification for an 'independent deterrent' is that the UK must be able to use it entirely alone without US approval. The Government makes the following three assurances:

> • "decision making and use of the system remains entirely sovereign to the UK; only the Prime Minister can authorise the launch of nuclear weapons, which ensures that political control is maintained at all times."
> • "the instruction to fire would be transmitted to the submarine using only UK codes and UK equipment; making the command and control procedures fully independent."
> • "our procurement relationship with the US regarding the *Trident* missile does not compromise the operational independence of our nuclear deterrent."[1]

All three beg the question as to whether the US can stop the UK from firing. The reality is that UK independence exists only so long as the US permits it. The Trident Commission – an authoritative, independent, cross-party inquiry which examined UK nuclear weapons policy – in its July 2014 Concluding Report stated that if the US withdrew support, UK 'independence' "would have a life expectancy measured in months".[2]

Dr Dan Plesch describes in considerable detail the extremely high level of UK dependence on the US, and the physical measures that the US could take to prevent a UK missile firing if it disapproved.[3] The missiles are maintained by, and leased from, a joint US-UK pool in Kings Bay, Georgia. The *Trident* replacement submarine missile tube module and its associated launch system is a joint project to be incorporated into the design of both the *Columbia* and *Dreadnought* class SSBNs. The onboard hardware and software systems to target

---

* See page 40 for references

the missiles are US supplied and maintained. Optimally they rely on US satellite-derived navigation and weather information for warhead guidance, albeit that less accurate fall-back systems can be used. Consequently the availability and use of the *Trident* weapon system is heavily reliant on US support and software skills. The warheads are notionally British, but US companies are deeply embedded in their design, and 70% of the company managing the Atomic Weapons Establishment (AWE) Aldermaston is US owned.[4] In sum, should the US wish to prevent the UK using *Trident*, it has the ability to do so.

Plesch points out that it is not inconceivable that the US, in the last resort, would consider military action to inhibit UK use. While this might seem incredible, the US was quite prepared to do so to stop the 1956 Anglo-French Suez campaign. General Sir Charles Keightley, UK Commander of Middle East Land Forces at the time, wrote afterwards: "It was the (military) action of the US which really defeated us in attaining our object." He complained that the actions of the US Sixth Fleet "endangered the whole of our relations with that country".[5]

In May 2019 there was a clear indication that the US is prepared to threaten reprisals on the UK if it does not comply with its wishes. The US Secretary of State, Mike Pompeo, warned that UK-US defence cooperation would be put at risk if the UK gave the Chinese company Huawei a role in operating the UK's 5G communication infrastructure.[6]

The Royal Navy (RN), Ministry of Defence (MoD) officials and Ministers all understand that maintaining the UK 'deterrent' as an effective weapon system is entirely dependent on US goodwill. As the former Prime Minister Tony Blair admitted in his autobiography: "[I]t is quite inconceivable that we would use our nuclear deterrent alone, without the US."[7] At a conference in June 2018, hosted by the National Museum of The Royal Navy, numerous RN and MoD speakers emphasised the dependence on the US for the effective operation of the UK *Trident* submarine force.

The illusion of an 'independent deterrent' is presented as fundamentally linked to UK permanent membership of the UN Security Council and thus a 'seat at the top table' as a major power. However, as one of the victors in World War II, the UK's membership was established before acquiring nuclear weapons; so this is irrelevant to its nuclear status. In support of one speaker's view at the 2019 Annual UK Project On Nuclear Issues (PONI) Conference that "UK possession of nuclear weapons has always been driven by the need for strong strategic links with the US", four recent occasions where the UK exactly shadowed the US position were pointed to. These were at conferences addressing the humanitarian impact of nuclear weapon use in Oslo (2013) and Vienna (2014), and the last two Nuclear Non-Proliferation Treaty (NPT) Review Conferences (2015, 2019).[8]

The Cost

In 2018 the total financial cost of replacing *Trident* was estimated at over £43Bn.[9] This makes the *Dreadnought* programme the second largest public capital procurement programme in the next decade, comparable only to the High Speed 2 railway line from London to Manchester and Leeds.

However, the full cost extends to the effect it has had on the operational capabilities of the Forces, and especially the RN. To accommodate this, the RN's conventional capabilities have been cut to the point where it would struggle to fulfil its historic core role of providing graduated conventional maritime deterrence. The current surface escort order of battle comprises six destroyers and 13 frigates – figures which match the six ships sunk in the Falklands War and 13 sufficiently damaged to put them out of action or severely limit their use. To put this in context, Rear Admiral Sir Sandy Woodward, the Operational Commander of all surface ships, land and air forces, stated: "During that time I lost nearly half of the destroyers and frigates I started with."[10] This was against a relatively limited enemy, engaging UK forces at long distance. Fortunately he had the numbers to absorb the high attrition rate. Similarly, on any given day only one, or possibly two, nuclear attack submarines are currently available – sometimes none – while the SSBN on Continuous At Sea Deterrence (CASD) deployment is a major liability requiring scarce ships and submarines to protect it as a very high value target. There is little or no provision for an attrition reserve today. Nelson famously said, "Were I to die at this moment, want of frigates would be found stamped on my heart."[11] Nothing has changed.

The financial and operational burdens of sustaining *Trident* are so great, and increasing, that they prejudice not just *Trident* renewal but the entire UK submarine-based nuclear weapons programme.[12] Some argue that this could be solved by moving the cost of renewing *Trident* back to the National Budget where it lay prior to 2010.[13] This would expose all the factors rehearsed here to the public, such that the political impact on the NHS and other social budgets would not be acceptable. So instead the Government has been putting more pressure on the Navy to find savings elsewhere.

The negative consequences of acquiring *Polaris*, and subsequently replacing it with *Trident*, were foreseen by two First Sea Lords. Admiral of the Fleet Sir Caspar John, First Sea Lord in 1964, on learning of the *Polaris* Sales Agreement, warned of the "millstone of *Polaris* hung around our necks" and as "potential wreckers of the real Navy." Admiral of the Fleet Sir Henry Leach echoed his predecessor's warning by describing the *Trident* programme as "the cuckoo in the nest".

As mentioned in Part 1, Vice Admiral Sir Jeremy Blackham, in his Foreword to Cdr Green's book *Security without Nuclear Deterrence*, correctly summed up the current situation: "But the cardinal point is that the nuclear deterrent is not and cannot be a substitute for conventional capabilities. The credibility of flexible response depends upon deferring any decision to use nuclear weapons until the very existence of the nation is at stake. This requirement means that the conventional forces must be of sufficient capability to deal with any lesser threat; and that one's potential enemy must believe this to be so." He further emphasised that "[i]f the conventional means at our disposal are weak, the point of transition to nuclear use may be lowered to levels at which the threat of nuclear obliteration is self-evidently wholly disproportionate ... At that point it is likely that deterrence through the threat of nuclear use becomes overtly incredible".[14]

Continuous at Sea Deterrence (CASD)

The Government states that "invulnerability and security of capability are key components of the credibility of our deterrent and contribute to overall stability."[15] CASD is a hangover from the Cold War's perceived need to be able to respond immediately if subjected to a 'bolt from the blue' attack from the USSR. This is why the *Polaris* force was kept at 15 minutes' notice to fire. No such need has existed since 1994 when UK and Russian strategic nuclear weapons were mutually detargeted;[16] and in 1998 the alert state of UK *Trident* was relaxed to several days' notice to fire, and has been ever since.[17]

Government studies confirm that a submarine-based missile

launching platform is currently the best of a range of options to deliver nuclear weapons.[18] The specific financial cost of ship, submarine and air assets employed to protect the CASD submarine cannot be obtained from MoD sources. Nonetheless, in defence of CASD it is argued that, in circumstances when an SSBN is not on patrol and an escalating threat requires it, the SSBNs are vulnerable to attack in harbour or in transit to deep water; also, the act of deployment exacerbates political tension.

However, it is hard to think of a realistic current scenario in which there is a need to respond to a threat of a 'bolt from the blue' nuclear attack on the UK or other NATO State. Long before circumstances reach the point where nuclear retaliation is the only option, there will be time to deploy an SSBN. Indeed, the act of doing so could be deliberately used as a further essential step up a political ladder of escalation. The Minister of State for the Armed Forces made this very point in evidence to a recent Parliamentary Inquiry on authorising the use of military force.[19] He was referring to 'boots on the ground', but the same logic applies to deploying naval or air assets.

UK Record on Nuclear Disarmament

The Nuclear Non-Proliferation Treaty (NPT) was signed in 1968 and came into force two years later. Article VI states: "Each of the Parties to the Treaty undertakes to pursue negotiations in good faith on effective measures relating to cessation of the nuclear arms race at an early date and to nuclear disarmament, and on a treaty on general and complete disarmament under strict and effective international control." There have been a number of recent five-yearly NPT reviews where the UK, in lock-step with the US and France, has opposed any measures to include reference to prohibiting and/or reducing its nuclear arsenals. At the conclusion of the May 2019 Preparatory Committee for the 2020 NPT Review Conference, four of the P5 (China was the exception) objected to several recommendations put forward by non-nuclear states such as "the need for a legally-binding norm to prohibit nuclear weapons in order to achieve and maintain a world without nuclear weapons."[20] In consequence they were not adopted.

The Chinese delegation, on the other hand, presented a remarkable and encouraging submission to the Preparatory Committee.[21] It included the following significant statements:

• "Countries possessing the largest nuclear arsenals bear special and primary responsibility for nuclear disarmament and should continue to make drastic and substantive reductions in their nuclear arsenals in a verifiable, irreversible and legally binding manner"; and
• "China undertakes not to be the first to use nuclear weapons at any time and under any circumstances."

The UK, on the other hand, refuses to rule out First Use. The implications of this on *Trident* submarine COs will be discussed in Part 3.

The lack of any significant progress in good faith towards the stated NPT goal of complete elimination of nuclear weapons drove 122 non-nuclear Member States of the UN General Assembly to negotiate a Treaty on the Prohibition of Nuclear Weapons (TPNW), which was adopted on 7 July 2017.[22] The NGO 'International Campaign to Abolish Nuclear Weapons' (ICAN) were awarded the 2017 Nobel Peace Prize in recognition of their outstanding work to help generate the political will to achieve this.[23] The TPNW requires ratification by 50 states to come into force.[24] While currently it is most unlikely that any nuclear-armed state will be among them, when the fiftieth state ratifies it, the Treaty's entry into force will significantly reinforce the growing international stigmatisation of nuclear deterrence. No doubt this is why the UK boycotted the TPNW negotiations and actively opposes the Treaty.[25]

Since the end of the Cold War the UK has taken the following nuclear disarmament steps:

• After the US and Russia mutually withdrew tactical nuclear weapons from surface ships and submarines in 1991, the UK followed suit a year later. By 1998, all WE.177 free fall nuclear bombs had been withdrawn from the RAF.[26]
• In 1994 PM John Major and Russian President Boris Yeltsin agreed to de-target their deployed strategic nuclear weapons. Subsequently, at the 2000 NPT Review Conference, all the P5 states confirmed that they had mutually de-targeted.[27]
• Reduction to a single nuclear weapon system (*Trident*).
• Reduction to a total of 220 nuclear warheads.
• The deployed SSBN's missiles reduced to eight, with a maximum of 40 warheads.[28]

The last three actions are taken on trust because they are not contained in any form of verifiable international agreement or protocol and so could be reversed at will. By contrast, the basis of US/USSR disarmament negotiations has always been 'trust but verify'.

The UK's 'main gate' decision to go ahead with the *Dreadnought* programme and new warhead ignores the disarmament obligation contained in Article VI of the NPT. It also sends a very hypocritical signal to (for example) North Korea: "We can be trusted to own and responsibly self-regulate our nuclear weapons as a deterrent, but you cannot."

Summary

The concept of an 'independent nuclear deterrent' is a political chimera. The US has the means, if it so wishes, to prevent the UK using its *Trident* weapon system. The financial and operational costs of sustaining *Trident* and the *Dreadnought* programme are unacceptably threatening the RN's historic core role of graduated conventional deterrence. UK *Trident* missiles have been detargeted since 1994; and since 1998 the deployed SSBN has been at a relaxed notice to fire of several days. With no realistic scenario of a 'bolt from the blue' nuclear threat, there is therefore no justification for maintaining CASD.

For over 20 years now, the UK has failed to pursue significant nuclear disarmament in good faith and has opposed the efforts of other states seeking to ban nuclear weapons. On the contrary, it is modernising its nuclear arsenal and delivery system. Unlike China, it keeps open the option to threaten first use of nuclear weapons, with serious implications for the SSBN command teams, which will be discussed in Part 3.

Part 3 – UK Nuclear Policy, International and Military Law, the UK Government's Position, and Consequences for *Trident* SSBN Commanding Officers*

From MAD to Non-Strategic Flexible Response (NSFR)

During the Cold War, the UK *Polaris* SSBN command teams understood that the policy of Mutually Assured Destruction (MAD) was based on a single premise. If the USSR launched a strategic nuclear strike against the UK or other NATO State, then the Prime Minister (PM) would authorise an order to respond with a retaliatory second strike. A deployed SSBN Commanding Officer (CO) could therefore make a pre-patrol judgement as to whether he felt he could justifiably and legally obey such an order. My CO and I were prepared to do this, because we had been briefed it would only be received if a nuclear attack was underway.[1] Though probably a futile last resort response, we accepted that such extreme circumstances would justify an act which probably contravened international humanitarian law, but which might still have prevented further launches by the USSR.

By contrast, in the late 1990s a new non-strategic option of variable numbers of low-yield warheads was incorporated into the existing 'Flexible Response' policy. For convenience I term this 'Non-Strategic Flexible Response' (NSFR); and it remains in force.[2] Designed to shore up the credibility of nuclear deterrence, it has much more complex implications for both the hostile State and the deployed SSBN CO. This was clarified in the run-up to the 2003 US-UK invasion of Iraq by the Secretary of State for Defence, Rt Hon Geoff Hoon MP: "The UK is prepared to use nuclear weapons against rogue states such as Iraq if they ever used weapons of mass destruction against British troops in the field."[3] The PM could now authorise first use – possibly with just a single low-yield warhead as a warning 'shot across the bow' – in support of deployed UK troops if they were subject to attack with chemical or biological weapons.[4] Ironically,

---

* See page 42 for references

these are banned internationally while nuclear weapons are not. No statement to deny, rescind or change this posture has been made since. This is deliberate, as MoD explained in this statement: "[W]e have neither a 'first use' nor a 'no first use' policy as it is essential that we do not simplify the calculations of our potential adversaries by defining exactly when, how and at what scale we would contemplate the use of our nuclear weapons."[5]

While the Government views *Trident* as a political weapon, and NSFR may be at a far lower destruction level than full-scale MAD, it opens up a raft of complex moral and legal questions, because NSFR is much closer to being a military action. Sir Michael Quinlan recognised the dangers of this: "[T]he Alliance's strategic concept of flexible response ... did not rule out first use or early use of nuclear weapons ... NATO authorities continually urged member countries ... to improve their contribution of conventional forces, so as to reduce the likelihood or rapidity of the Alliance's having to confront such hugely difficult options."[6]

Ambiguity is designed to create uncertainty for threatening States. However, this also affects the SSBN CO, because he needs to assess the situation in relation to international law, especially as the legal norms governing the threat or use of nuclear weapons have been significantly strengthened since the Cold War ended. More importantly, although the PM authorises weapon release, he or she does not 'press the nuclear button'. The SSBN CO has this ultimate responsibility by turning his 'Captain's Key' to give permission to fire.

US Developments in Nuclear Posture

In 2018, a new US *Nuclear Posture Review* included the following statement: "Expanding flexible U.S. nuclear options now, to include low-yield options, is important to preserve credible deterrence against regional aggression".[7] To implement this, in June 2019 the Pentagon released joint nuclear planning guidance, including this claim: "Employment of nuclear weapons can radically alter or accelerate the course of a campaign. A nuclear weapon could be brought into the campaign as a result of perceived failure in a conventional campaign, potential loss of control or regime, or to escalate the conflict to sue for peace on more favourable terms. The potential consequences of using nuclear weapons will greatly influence military operations".[8] First use of low-yield warheads could constitute nuclear warfighting which arguably lowers the nuclear threshold. Because of UK nuclear dependence on the US, the Government will probably come under pressure to support and emulate it.

Prompted by widespread concerns following US President Donald Trump's nuclear threats to North Korea's President Kim Jong-un, in February 2019 the Middlebury Institute of International Studies at Monterey, a US think tank of similar status to Chatham House, published a report comparing who is authorised to initiate the use of nuclear weapons and procedures in each of the nine nuclear-armed States.[9] It includes reports that US SSBN COs are expected to challenge an unexpected launch order that seems out of place or character, and refers to recent public statements by current and ex-Chiefs of US Strategic Command that they would challenge an illegal firing order.

International Law

An overview follows of the main legal instruments governing the Law of Armed Conflict applicable to the threat or use of nuclear weapons. The UK, along with the other permanent members of the UN Security Council (known as the P5), has to varying degrees adopted legal positions on them which are strongly disputed by many respected international lawyers and the overwhelming majority of non-nuclear weapon States. Thus, the deployed SSBN CO should not accept compliance as a given without knowing all the factors behind an order to launch.

Additional Protocol 1 (AP1) to the 1949 Geneva Conventions is a treaty negotiated at an International Conference chaired by the International Committee of the Red Cross which came into force in December 1978. AP1 enshrines the principles of proportionality[10] and distinction[11] for the protection of civilians and civilian objects. At the insistence of the P5, there was no discussion as to which weapons might breach these rules; but this did not mean that the Conference agreed they were exempt. Nonetheless, on ratifying AP1 in 1998, the UK attached a reservation asserting that the rules introduced by it apply only to conventional, not nuclear, weapons.[12] However, as the International Court of Justice (ICJ) emphasised in its 1996 Advisory Opinion on the Threat or Use of Nuclear Weapons, all States are bound by the rules in AP1 which are merely the expression of pre-existing customary law.[13]

When asked for the basis for the UK Reservation, the MoD replied that the 1977 Conference "did not discuss the legality of nuclear weapons."[14] This is correct because AP1 focuses on the rules, not what might breach them. The reservation is cited in the advice given to military commanders in *The Joint Service Manual of The Law of Armed Conflict (JSP383)* as a purported justification for the use of nuclear weapons.[15]

The 1996 ICJ Advisory Opinion was given in response to a UN General Assembly question: "Is the threat or use of nuclear weapons in any circumstance permitted under international law?" The ICJ decided that "the threat or use of nuclear weapons would generally be contrary to the rules of international law applicable in armed conflict." However, it could not "conclude definitively whether the threat or use of nuclear weapons would be lawful or unlawful in an extreme circumstance of self-defence, in which the very survival of a State would be at stake."[16] The clear implication is that in any circumstances other than an existential nuclear weapon attack on the UK, the use of nuclear weapons in response would indisputably be unlawful. Regarding the *in extremis* uncertainty, the ICJ President emphasised that this did not mean that the ICJ was "leaving the door ajar to recognition of the legality of the threat or use of nuclear weapons."[17]

The Rome Statute of 1998 establishing the International Criminal Court (ICC) states: "Intentionally launching an attack in the knowledge that such attack will cause incidental loss of life or injury to civilians or damage to civilian objects or widespread, long-term and severe damage to the natural environment which would be clearly excessive in relation to the concrete and direct overall military advantage anticipated" is a war crime within the ICC's jurisdiction.[18] When ratifying it, the UK drew the Court's attention to its reservation to AP1; but the Rome Statute prohibits reservations, so its war crime provisions are unaffected and therefore the threat or use of nuclear weapons is not excluded from the ICC's jurisdiction.

Reference to the environment is of added significance in light of recent updated research on the effect of extended nuclear warfighting in South Asia, which found that the smoke alone from firestorms would cause sufficient temperature drop to lead to global famine.[19]

2017 Treaty on the Prohibition of Nuclear Weapons (TPNW). Frustrated by lack of P5 compliance with their disarmament obligations in the 1968 Nuclear Non-Proliferation Treaty (NPT), to date 80 non-nuclear weapon States have signed the TPNW, 47 have ratified it and others are in process.[20] As mentioned in Part 2, the P5 boycotted the negotiations and have refused to sign the Treaty. Nonetheless, once the necessary 50 States have ratified, its entry into force will further stigmatise the threat or use of nuclear weapons and show that non-nuclear weapon States are prepared to hold nuclear armed states accountable.[21] This trend will intensify as evidence emerges that the US is planning to modernise *Trident* missiles to sustain deployment in the *Columbia* class SSBNs through to the 2080s.[22]

Joint Service Manual of the Law of Armed Conflict (JSP 383)

JSP 383 states that the legality of nuclear weapon use "depends upon the application of the general rules of international law, including those regulating the use of force and the conduct of hostilities."[23] Against this general statement military commanders must then test the specific circumstances in which they receive a launch order to decide whether they can lawfully obey it. The following extracts from JSP 383 define the tests that must be applied:

Level of Responsibility

"Those who plan or decide upon attacks are the planners and commanders and they have a duty to verify targets, take precautions to reduce incidental damage, and refrain from attacks that offend the proportionality principle. Whether a person will have this responsibility will depend on whether he has any discretion in the way the attack is carried out and so the responsibility will range from commanders-in-chief and their planning staff to single soldiers opening fire on their own initiative."[24]

Comment: As already mentioned, an SSBN CO has discretion, granting or withholding permission to fire by use of the 'Captain's Key' available only to them. International Criminal Court Article 33 states that they are under a duty not to obey a manifestly unlawful order.[25]

Proportionality

"[C]ivilian immunity does not make unlawful the unavoidable

expected incidental civilian casualties and damage which may result from legitimate attacks upon military objectives, *provided that the incidental casualties and damage are not excessive in relation to the concrete and direct military advantage anticipated.* This is the principle of proportionality."[26] (emphasis added)

Comment: The need to observe proportionality is the subject of a Chatham House Research Paper.[27] In the open forum following its launch, I asked whether the principle of proportionality applied to nuclear weapons, and how an SSBN CO could make a judgement on this. A former RN officer on the panel who had served in a legal capacity in the MoD's Nuclear Policy Department avoided my question, claiming that the UK always complies with international law, implying that the SSBN CO could therefore unquestioningly trust the PM's authorisation.

Distinction/Discrimination

"The principle of distinction separates those who may be legitimately the subject of direct attack, namely combatants and those who take a direct part in hostilities, from those who may not be so subject. It also separates legitimate targets, namely military objectives, from civilian objects. This principle, and its application to warfare, is given expression in Additional Protocol 1 1977."[28]

Comment: While JSP 383 references the 1998 Rome Statute, it does not comment on how the use of nuclear weapons would be treated by the ICC in the same way that it comments on AP1.

Because of their indiscriminate nature, it is difficult to see how nuclear weapons could be used without violating these principles. At the very least, to meet the criteria of JPS 383, the SSBN CO would need details of the assigned targets and expected effects on military objectives and civilians to be able to make an informed decision. However, unless the circumstances had arisen before going on patrol when access to planners and legal advice could be obtained, it is most unlikely that the CO would be able to communicate with them once on patrol.

Therefore, the advice given to SSBN COs in JSP 383 should not be accepted without question if first use is ordered.

The UK no longer accepts the ICJ's jurisdiction regarding nuclear weapons

In February 2017, the UK repudiated the authority of the ICJ in contentious cases concerning nuclear weapons following the Court's judgment in a case brought by the Marshall Islands concerning the obligation to negotiate in good faith towards nuclear disarmament. The UK amended its declaration recognising the jurisdiction of the Court by excluding "any claim or dispute that arises from or is connected with or related to nuclear disarmament and/or nuclear weapons, unless all of the other nuclear-weapon States Party to the Treaty on the Non-Proliferation of Nuclear Weapons have also consented to the jurisdiction of the Court and are party to the proceedings in question."[29]

This 'opt out' effectively removed the UK from the ICJ's jurisdiction over contentious cases involving nuclear weapons, but it does not affect the Court's advisory jurisdiction. It can only be interpreted as a defensive measure in the face of increasing international legal objections to the threat or use of nuclear weapons. This, together with the reservation attached to AP1, undermines the PM's statement that "we need to stand up for the global rules and standards that keep us safe" made in the 2018 Parliamentary debate justifying bombing a Syrian chemical warfare facility.[30] The need to observe a rules-based system is also frequently cited in the 2018 *National Security Capability Review.*[31]

The Good Operation. MoD handbook for military planners

Published by the MoD in 2017 following the Chilcot Inquiry into the 2003 US-UK Iraq invasion, the handbook reiterates the Government's assertion that it complies at all times with international law, and that legal advice to military commanders is in JSP 383.[32] However, if its advice is followed, it is hard to see how first use of nuclear weapons could possibly be considered lawful.

Public Administration and Constitutional Affairs Select Committee (PACAC) Inquiry: Authorising the Use of Military Force

Mindful of these findings, I made a written submission to this apposite and timely Inquiry, convened to examine how to implement the Chilcot Report's recommendation that Parliament should be more involved in a decision to go to war [see Chapter III]. It took evidence from senior Government representatives, military, academics and members of the public between 12 March and 20 May 2019.[33] My submission was accepted, and reference was made to it in oral questions to two specialists in constitutional codes and practices. They were surprised to learn that the UK might launch *Trident* in circumstances other than as a retaliatory second strike.[34] Another witness, Admiral Lord West, First Sea Lord during the 2003 Iraq invasion, supported the thrust of my submission of which he had received a copy, expressing concern that SSBN COs should not "be held responsible for taking illegal action in international law" and that this should be rectified.[35]

Parts 1-3 Conclusions

The absence of major war between nuclear armed states probably owes more to avoidance of inadvertent or mistaken use, or sheer luck, than nuclear deterrence. What is undisputed is that the financial and operational costs of sustaining *Trident* have dangerously degraded the RN's core role of providing graduated conventional maritime deterrence. This has created an ironic counter-reality to the political mantra that "the UK's independent nuclear deterrent keeps us safe".

The Government's determination to sustain its nuclear weapon capability has less to do with guaranteeing UK security than a desire to maintain its status as a P5 member, sustain strong strategic links with the US, and avoid France becoming the sole European nuclear power. Although successive Governments have claimed nuclear independence from the US, the UK's nuclear capability relies heavily upon US goodwill and technical expertise, and entails uncritical support of US foreign policy. Furthermore, since mutual de-targeting of UK and Russian warheads in 1994, followed by relaxing the notice to fire of UK *Trident* to several days in 1998, Continuous At Sea

Deterrence no longer makes operational sense, and amounts to misemployment of scarce military assets for contentious political purposes.

The UK's current option of 'Non-Strategic Flexible Response' embraces first use with low-yield warheads against military threats well short of existential homeland defence. Moreover, the UK will probably come under pressure to support and emulate recent disturbing US developments reviving nuclear warfighting. Contravening military and international humanitarian law, these changes introduce uncertainty for the SSBN CO, who (unlike the PM) has the ultimate responsibility of initiating missile launch. Despite claims of championing a rules-based international order, the Government has resorted to dubious declarations to avoid legal compliance, which will become increasingly untenable following entry into force of the 2017 Treaty on the Prohibition of Nuclear Weapons. This could place SSBN COs in legal and moral jeopardy, not least because Nuremberg Principle IV states that unquestioning obedience to a superior's order is not enough.

Acknowledgement: Professor Nick Grief of the University of Kent has provided invaluable advice on matters of international law; but, in the end, all opinions and facts are entirely my responsibility.

Postscript to Parts 1–3
The Law – and Moral Responsibility
(October 2020)

Since publication of the three previous articles I have received more feedback in support than against; but one critique in particular led to an extensive exchange of views on a public website with a former Assistant Chief of Defence Staff (Nuclear, Chemical & Biological), Rear Admiral John Gower. We disagreed in several areas, but we did both object to first use and ambiguity of use and agreed that the sole purpose of nuclear weapons should be to deter/counter the use of nuclear weapons. However, we then disagreed on how to change Government policy. I would like to see the Government unilaterally set aside its ambiguity and adopt a policy of 'no first use' as, say, China has done and also 'sole use' against a nuclear attack; whereas Adm Gower believes this should all be part of multi-lateral negotiations between the nuclear powers.

He also answered the question I posed in Part 3 of my series – how can a *Trident* CO know that he is not in breach of the laws of armed conflict or international humanitarian law when he does not know the facts? His response was:

> "[I]t has long been recognised that the SSBN CO on distant patrol cannot under any circumstances have access to the range of factors necessary in determining either the necessity or the legality of a launch of his missiles. That the decision to launch is taken by the highest political leadership, with the advice of the broad church of political and legal bodies fully cognisant of their legal responsibilities has removed, uniquely in military commands, this responsibility from his shoulders."

If he is correct (MoD has declined to confirm – see pp. 36-38), some fundamental consequences and questions arise:

1. The SSBN CO, like every serviceman or woman, is under a duty not to obey a manifestly unlawful order. This is reflected in Article 33 of the Rome Statute, which concerns the defence of superior orders.

2. According to Principle IV of the Principles of International Law recognised in the Charter and Judgment of the Nuremberg Tribunal, the fact that a person acted pursuant to order of his Government or of a superior does not relieve him or her from responsibility under international law, provided a moral choice was in fact possible.

3. Military law states that a military commander with the ability to withhold fire, as a *Trident* CO has, must make a decision as to whether an order to fire complies with international law.

4. If an SSBN CO is legally absolved from these responsibilities and in the absence of any clear Government policy excluding 'first use', what assurance do *Trident* COs have that they will never be ordered to comply with an unlawful order? Is the statement that "the Government always complies with international law" sufficient? This requires them to place unquestioning trust in the Prime Minister – but remember Iraq and Prime Minister Blair, and at least one former *Trident* CO has stated he would not trust Prime Minister Johnson.[1]

It is my assertion that the Government's failure to make clear how its nuclear weapons may be employed – i.e. the policy of deliberate ambiguity – places COs in an impossible moral position.

They will be well aware of the requirements of international law, of *Trident's* immense destructive power, and hence of the very high risk of unlawful use. Even if the letter of the law absolves them from legal responsibility for obeying a launch order, they must still make a moral judgement as to whether they are prepared to launch in circumstances of which they have no specific knowledge nor know the limits within which the Prime Minister can authorise launch. Furthermore, Admiral Gower has stated that the military would not be involved in the decision to launch:

> "The UK is significantly different from all other nuclear weapon states in that the military has no formal role in the advice or decision upon whether to launch UK SLBM (save detailed expert advice on whether the options for consideration are capable of being executed as the political leadership might desire)."[2]

COs are therefore denied any assurance of approval from their military superiors. Against this background, notwithstanding their legal position, and given the fallibility of politicians, can COs confidently place their moral trust in a potentially fallible Prime Minister? One must also question why the UK is significantly different from all other nuclear weapon states.

From my own knowledge while serving in the *Polaris* Force, COs and their second in command Executive Officers, (the other half of the two-person launch authorisation team) could make such moral judgements prior to accepting their command appointments, knowing that they would be ordered to launch solely in retaliation for a nuclear attack on UK/NATO. Not all could accept even this limitation as to use and so declined to take command. No such clear understanding exists today. It should.

Annexe to Postscript
An Exchange of Letters

Director General Nuclear Secretariat
MoD Main Building
London
SW1A 2HB

9 January 2020

Dear Director General

In correspondence with your Directorate between November 2017 and December 2018, I sought to establish how a *Trident* SSBN Commanding Officer (CO) on receipt of a fire order could be confident that he is not being ordered to commit genocide or a crime against humanity as the *Joint Services Manual of Law of Armed Conflict (JSP383)* requires of him. Furthermore, Nuremberg Principles IV and VII and Article 33 of the Rome Statute of the International Criminal Court (ICC) also place direct responsibility on the CO not to obey an order which is manifestly unlawful even though it emanates from a superior. Therefore, in order to be sure that he is acting lawfully, he needs to know the details of his targets and the effects of his weapons on them. As you will see from our correspondence, my concern grew out of a realisation that the CO is as much subject to the deliberate ambiguity of Government nuclear weapon policy regarding first use, targets and number of warheads as the intended target(s).

Your Directorate did not provide an answer to this other than stating in a variety of different ways that Government policy is lawful. When I pressed further your Directorate terminated the correspondence.

Rear Admiral John Gower (retired former ACDS Nuclear, Chemical & Biological), writing in response to my comments dated 25 November 2019 on his article UK: Nuclear Weapon Command, Control and Communications published on 12 September 2019 on the public website www.nautilus.org, stated:

"…[T]hat the SSBN command has no knowledge of the targets

which the PM has ordered selected absolves them of the Nuremberg Principles, which are based on the simple fact that a subordinate subject to them has knowledge of the specifics of the order and discretion in carrying them out. Continued legal advice supports this."

Does Rear Admiral Gower's interpretation of the Nuremberg Principles in relation to ICC Article 33 accurately reflect the Government's position and, if so, can your Directorate provide details of this legal advice?

Yours sincerely

Robert Forsyth

* * * *

Ministry of Defence

Our Ref: TO2020/00420

Your Ref:

Commander (Rtd) Forsyth

Ministry of Defence
Main Building
Whitehall
London SW1A 2HB
United Kingdom

| Telephone: | +44(0)20 7218 9000 |
| E-mail: | DNO-SecretariatTeam@mod.gov.uk |

13 February 2020

Dear Commander Forsyth,

Thank you for your most recent letter, dated 9 January 2020, regarding comments made by Rear Admiral John Gower (Rtd) in relation to the legal standing of a submarine commander given the order to fire a *Trident* missile.

Rear Admiral Gower, since he has retired from the Royal Navy, is not a Government spokesperson and is entitled to express his own views as he wishes, whether they are in agreement or not with the Government's position.

In our previous correspondence we have outlined the Government's position on various aspects relating to the legality of the nuclear deterrent and the use of our nuclear weapons should we ever be required to do so. This position has not changed. While we do not intend to repeat all of that previous detail here, we will summarise again the key points.

We hope never to employ nuclear weapons but to deliver a deterrent effect under all circumstances. We would only consider using our nuclear weapons in the most extreme circumstances of self-defence, including the defence of our NATO allies.

The Government is clear that the use of nuclear weapons – like all weapons – would be subject to the requirements of international law. The 1996 International Court of Justice Advisory Opinion could not reach a definitive conclusion on the legality or illegality of the use of nuclear weapons by a state in an extreme circumstance of self-defence, in which its very survival would be at stake. It concluded that legality could only be determined in light of the specific circumstances applying when such use is being contemplated and the application of the general rules of law, particularly those regulating the use of force and the conduct of hostilities. Should the circumstances arise in which use of nuclear weapons needs to be considered, legal aspects would be a contributing factor in the decision-making process.

In our last letter to you, dated 7 November 2018, we suggested that, while we appreciate that you hold strong views on this matter, further correspondence would serve no purposeful outcome as we had already written to you on several occasions. There is no further information to add on this topic beyond what has already been communicated to you. Therefore, no further purpose will be served by continuing the correspondence.

Yours sincerely,

Defence Nuclear Organisation Secretariat

References

Part 1: The Concept of Nuclear Deterrence

1. Generally referred to as 'The Moscow Criterion'.
2. UK Strategic Defence Review 1998. para 68, accessed at https://webarchive.nationalarchives.gov.uk/20121018172816/http:/www.mod.uk/NR/rdonlyres/65F3D7AC-4340-4119-93A2-20825848E50E/0/sdr1998_complete.pdf
3. Nuclear Weapon Non-Proliferation Treaty (NPT) 1968, accessed at https://www.un.org/disarmament/wmd/nuclear/npt/text
4. Parliamentary Debate UK's Nuclear Deterrent, 18 July 2016, Hansard, accessed at https://hansard.parliament.uk/Commons/2016-07-18/debates/7B7A196B-B37C-4787-99DC-098882B3EFA2/UKSNuclearDeterrent)%20Column%20568
5. Correspondence between Cdr Forsyth and MoD Nuclear Policy Department, see later sections of this book.
6. Hennessy, Peter, *Cabinets and the Bomb* (Oxford University Press, 2007). The initial decision to acquire nuclear weapons was influenced by Labour Foreign Secretary Ernest Bevin in 1946 declaring to Attlee's Cabinet that "we've got to have a bloody Union Jack on it" (p.8); and a subsequent fear of France being the sole European nuclear power sustains this.
7. Blair, Tony, *A Journey: My Political Life* (Random House, 2010).
8. Shultz, George P. & Goodby, James E. Ed., *The War That Must Never Be Fought: Dilemmas of Nuclear Deterrence* (Hoover Institution Press, 2015), accessed at https://www.hoover.org/research/war-must-never-be-fought
9. *Wikipedia*, 'USS Growler', accessed at https://en.wikipedia.org/wiki/USS_Growler_(SSG-577)
10. *Wikipedia*, 'Vasily Arkhipov (Vice Admiral)', accessed at https://en.wikipedia.org/wiki/Vasily_Arkhipov_(vice_admiral)
11. Yuri Andropov & Averill Harriman in conversation, 'The 1983 War Scare: "The Last Paroxysm" of the Cold War Part 1', accessed at https://nsarchive2.gwu.edu/NSAEBB/NSAEBB426/
12. Lewis, Patricia, Williams, Heather, Pelopidas, Benoit and Aghlani, Sasan, Too Close for Comfort: Cases of Near Nuclear Use and Options for Policy (Chatham House Report, The Royal Institute of International Affairs, April 2014), accessed at https://www.chathamhouse.org/sites/default/files/field/field_document/20140428TooCloseforComfortNuclearUseLewisWilliamsPelopidasAghlani.pdf
13. FAQs related to the Ballistic Missile False Alert 13 January 2018, accessed at https://dod.hawaii.gov/hiema/faqs-related-to-the-ballistic-missile-false-alert/
14. Braithwaite, Rodric, *Armageddon & Paranoia: The Nuclear Confrontation* (Profile Books, 2017) p.355.
15. Ibid.
16. Ibid, p.186.

17. Green, Robert, *Security without Nuclear Deterrence* (Spokesman Books, 2018). Foreword, p.19.

18. Ibid.

Part 2: A Review of UK Nuclear Weapon Policy

1. HM Government Policy Paper, The UK's nuclear deterrent: what you need to know, 19 February 2018, accessed at https://www.gov.uk/government/publications/uk-nuclear-deterrence-factsheet/uk-nuclear-deterrence-what-you-need-to-know%20

2. British American Security Council , *Trident Commission Final Report,* July 2014, accessed at https://www.basicint.org/

3. Dr Dan Plesch with John Ainslie, Trident: Strategic Dependence & Sovereignty (SOAS, University of London, 2016), accessed at https://www.soas.ac.uk/cisd/news/file114165.pdf

4. Nuclear Information Service (NIS) Report, *AWE: Britain's Nuclear Weapon Factory – Past, Present and Possibilities for the Future,* June 2016, https://nuclearinfo.org/sites/default/files/AWE-Past%2C%20Present%2C%20Future%20Report%202016.pdf

5. Peter Hitchens, Daily Mail, 15 June 2014, accessed at https://www.dailymail.co.uk/debate/article-2657873/Uncovered-American-duplicity-finally-explodes-myth-Special-Relationship-How-US-discussed-blasting-hell-UK-forces-Suez-Crisis-shameful-betrayals-historic-alliance.html

6. Tom Belger, 'U.S secretary of state Pompeo threatens Britain over Huawei 5G row', *Yahoo Finance UK*, 9 May 2019, accessed at https://uk.finance.yahoo.com/news/pompeo-threatens-to-stop-sharing-intelligence-with-uk-over-huawei-5-g-row-144154421.html?guce_referrer=aHR0cHM6Ly93d3cuZ29vZ2xlLmNvbS8&guce_referrer_sig=AQAAAEbMryPunnqF6BzhBLu7r0Nl0ViX50ro-LLuvL5_s5modkpLv0U5bh-80cVdCkzRs0ynNrZuasiEd54Tbnfe25ithpD7YOkVvnUcmEP0QRsl4UUFAbsBo4EzX0Zx1PuxRu3Wbp8szznTXyRwqKbvmNvH82ENN0k9nWJOh0LO7Tw4&_guc_consent_skip=1597658962

7. Tony Blair, *A Journey* (Hutchinson, London, 2010), p.636.

8. Jana Wattenberg, Aberystwyth University, presentation at RUSI PONI Annual Conference, 13 June 2019, , starting at 00.38, accessed at https://www.nuclearreactions.rusi.org/single-post/2019/07/30/UK-PONI-Conference-2019-A-Summary

9. British American Security Council Report, Blowing up the Budget, 2018, accessed at https://basicint.org/report-blowing-up-the-budget/

10. Admiral Sandy Woodward, *One Hundred days* (Harper Collins, London, 1992), Epilogue, p.348.

11. Exclaimed in frustration after the battle of the Nile, Aug. 1, 1798, being unable

to pursue the enemy for want of frigates.

12. Nuclear Information Service Report, *Trouble Ahead*, 29 April 2019, accessed at https://basicint.org/article/nis-reports/new-report-trouble-ahead

13. Save the Royal Navy, *Has the time come to the move the cost of Trident replacement out of the MoD budget*, 27 November 2017, accessed at https://basicint.org/report-blowing-up-the-budget/

14. Commander Robert Green, Royal Navy (Ret'd), *Security without Nuclear Deterrence* (Spokesman Books, Nottingham, 2018) Foreword p.17.

15. HM Government Policy Paper, *The UK's nuclear deterrent: what you need to know*, 19 February 2018, accessed at https://www.gov.uk/government/publications/uk-nuclear-deterrence-factsheet/uk-nuclear-deterrence-what-you-need-to-know

16. Christopher Bellamy, 'Britain stops pointing its missiles at Russia', Independent, 3 June 1994.

17. Select Committee on Defence Eighth Report 20 June 2006, 2. *The UK's Strategic Nuclear Deterrent*. The 1998 Strategic Defence Review, para. 40.

18. HM Government, *Trident Alternatives Review*, 16 July 2013, Executive Summary, para. 32, accessed at https://www.gov.uk/government/publications/trident-alternatives-review

19. RT Hon Mark Lancaster, Minister for the Armed Forces, Oral Evidence to PACAC Inquiry Authorising the use of Military Force, 20 May 2019, in answer to Q.243, accessed at http://data.parliament.uk/writtenevidence/committeeevidence.svc/evidencedocument/public-administration-and-constitutional-affairs-committee/the-role-of-parliament-in-the-uk-constitution-authorising-the-use-of-military-force/oral/102462.pdf

20. Dr Joseph Gerson, 'Human Survival Lies in the Balance as the Charade of NPT Diplomacy is Wearing Thin', In Depth News, 16 May 2019, accessed at https://www.indepthnews.net/index.php/armaments/nuclear-weapons/2689-human-survival-lies-in-the-balance-as-the-charade-of-npt-diplomacy-is-wearing-thin

21. Statement by Chinese Delegation at the Third Session of the Preparatory Committee for the 2020 NPT Review Conference on Nuclear Disarmament, 2 May 2019.

22. UN Office for Disarmament Affairs, Treaty on the Prohibition of Nuclear Weapons 2017.

23. ICAN Nobel Peace Prize, 6 October 2017, see https://icanw.org/

24. ICAN: Status of the Treaty to Prohibit Nuclear Weapons, see https://icanw.org/

25. UK statement on treaty prohibiting nuclear weapons, 8 July 2017, accessed at https://www.gov.uk/government/news/uk-statement-on-treaty-prohibiting-nuclear-weapons%20

26. WE.177, Wikipedia, accessed at https://en.wikipedia.org/wiki/WE.177

27. Statement by the delegations of France, the People's Republic of China, the Russian Federation, the United Kingdom of Great Britain and Northern Ireland and

the United States of America, Review Conference of the Parties to the Treaty on the Non-Proliferation of Nuclear Weapons, NPT/CONF/2000/21, 1 May 2000.

28. HM Government Policy Paper, The UK's nuclear deterrent: what you need to know, 19 February 2018, accessed at https://www.gov.uk/government/publications/uk-nuclear-deterrence-factsheet/uk-nuclear-deterrence-what-you-need-to-know

Part 3: UK Nuclear Weapon Policy, International and Military Law, the UK Government's Position, and Consequences for *Trident* SSBN Commanding Officers

1. As Executive Officer, Starboard Crew, HMS Repulse 1970-72

2. Professor Paul Rogers, Memorandum to Select Committee on Defence, 15 January 2007

3. Evidence to the Parliamentary Defence Select Committee, 20 March 2002

4. Professor Paul Rogers, Britain's Other Nuclear Weapons, openDemocracy, 22 March 2018, accessed at https://www.opendemocracy.net/en/britains-other-nuclear-weapons/

5. MoD letter to the author, 7 November 2018

6. Michael Quinlan, *Thinking about Nuclear Weapons: Principles, Problems, Prospects* (Oxford University Press, 2009), p. 35

7. US Nuclear Posture Review, February 2018, *Enhancing Deterrence with Non-Strategic Nuclear Capabilities*, p.XII, accessed at https://dod.defense.gov/News/Special-Reports/0218_npr/. By low-yield the Trump Administration means less than 10 kilotons – see Congressional Research Service, *A Low-Yield Submarine-Launched Nuclear Warhead: Overview of the Expert Debate*, 21 March 2019, accessed at https://fas.org/sgp/crs/nuke/IF11143.pdf

8. Joint Chiefs of Staff Joint Publication 3-72, Nuclear Operations, 11 June 2019, Chapter V, p. V-3, para 3e, accessed at https://fas.org/irp/doddir/dod/jp3_72.pdf

9. Jeffrey G. Lewis and Bruno Tertrais, *The Finger on the Button: The Authority to Use Nuclear Weapons in Nuclear-Armed States*, Middlebury Institute of International Studies at Monterey, James Martin Center for Non-proliferation Studies Occasional Paper 45, February 2019, accessed at https://www.nonproliferation.org/wp-content/uploads/2019/02/Finger-on-the-Nuclear-Button.pdf

10. AP1 Article 51(5)(b) prohibits "…an attack which may be expected to cause incidental loss of civilian life, injury to civilians, damage to civilian objects, or a combination thereof, which would be excessive in relation to the concrete and direct military advantage anticipated." Article 85(3)(b) regards as a grave breach of this Protocol "…launching an indiscriminate attack affecting the civilian population or civilian objects in the knowledge that such attack will cause excessive loss of life, injury to civilians or damage to civilian objects, as defined in Article 57, paragraph 2 a) iii)"

11. AP1 Article 48: "In order to ensure respect for and protection of the civilian population and civilian objects, the Parties to the conflict shall at all times distinguish between the civilian population and combatants and between civilian objects and military objectives and accordingly shall direct their operations only against military objectives".

12. UK Reservation on ratifying AP1 to Geneva Conventions, 28 January 1998.

13. International Court of Justice Advisory Opinion, *Legality of the Threat or Use of Nuclear Weapons*, 8 July 1996, para. 84.

14. MoD letter to the author, 7 November 2018.

15. Amended up to and including May 2013.

16. International Court of Justice Advisory Opinion 1996, para. 105.2(E).

17. Judge Bedjaoui, ICJ President, Declaration on pronouncing Advisory Opinion, 8 July 1996, para. 11.

18. Rome Statute of the International Criminal Court, Article 8 (2)(b)(iv).

19. Alan Robock et al, *Nuclear winter revisited with a modern climate model and current nuclear arsenals: Still catastrophic consequences*, Journal of Geophysical Research, Vol 112, 6 July 2007.

20. International Campaign to Abolish Nuclear Weapons, 'Signature/ratification status of the Treaty on the Prohibition of Nuclear Weapons,' and 'Progress towards Ratification', see https://icanw.org

21. The TPNW will enter into force 90 days after the fiftieth instrument of ratification, acceptance, approval or accession has been deposited.

22. Megan Eckstein, 'Navy Beginning Tech Study to Extend Trident Nuclear Missiles into the 2080s', USNI News, 14 November 2019, accessed at https://news.usni.org/2019/11/14/navy-beginning-tech-study-to-extend-trident-nuclear-missile-into-the-2080s

23. JSP 383 para. 6.17.

24. Ibid, para. 5.32.9.

25. Nuremberg Principle IV states: "The fact that a person acted pursuant to order of his government or superior does not relieve him from responsibility under international law, provided a moral choice was in fact possible for him."

26. JSP383, para. 2.4.2.

27. https://www.chathamhouse.org/sites/default/files/publications/research/2018

28. JSP 383, para 2.5.1.

29. Sir Alan Duncan, Minister of State for Foreign and Commonwealth Affairs, *Amendments to the UK's Optional Clause Declaration to the International Court of Justice: Written Statement HCWS489*, 23 February 2017.

30. Prime Minister's statement on Syria, House of Commons, 16 April 2018, Column 44.

31. HM Government, *National Security Capability Review*, March 2018.

32. MoD, The Good Operation: A handbook for those involved in operational policy and its implementation, January 2018.

33. Written submission by the author to PACAC Inquiry.

34. Professor Gavin Philipson & Dr James Strong in oral evidence to PACAC Inquiry, 12 March 2019, answers to Questions 79-88.

35. Oral Evidence by Senior Military Officers to PACAC Inquiry, 26 March 2019, answers to Questions 157 -158.

Postscript to Parts 1-3

1. Dr Andrew Corbett (former *Trident* submarine CO) 20 July 20202: https://bylinetimes.com/2020/07/20/i-wouldnt-want-to-press-the-nuclear-button-for-boris-johnson/

2. Rear Admiral John Gower writing on the Nautilus Institute website. 12 September 2019. https://nautilus.org/napsnet/napsnet-special-reports/united-kingdom-nuclear-weapon-command-control-and-communications/

CHAPTER III

Chilcot, Trident and Jeopardy

Papers submitted to the Public Administration and Constitutional Affairs Committee Inquiry: 'The Role of Parliament in the UK Constitution: Authorising the Use of Military Force', February 2019

Re-Targetting Trident – Parliament should be involved

Executive Summary

In 1994 the five permanent members of the UN Security Council mutually agreed to de-target their nuclear weapons. This paper lays out the reasons why the findings of the Chilcot Enquiry have made it mandatory that Parliament is directly involved in any proposals to re-target UK's *Trident* missiles. Failure to do so could place the Prime Minister and *Trident* submarine Commanding Officers in legal and moral jeopardy.

Background

1. Arguably, the Cold War ended for the Royal Navy in February 1994 when UK Prime Minister John Major and Russian President Boris Yeltsin signed an agreement mutually to de-target their deployed strategic nuclear weapons, echoing an agreement by US President Bill Clinton and Yeltsin a month earlier.[1] Britain's nuclear posture was further relaxed in 1998, when the Labour Government announced in its Strategic Defence Review that *"our submarines routinely are at a notice to fire measured in days"*, thereby removing the immediate threat of destruction from many Russian cities. At the 2000 Nuclear Non-Proliferation Treaty (NPT) Review Conference, all five permanent members of the UN Security Council confirmed that they had mutually de-targeted. The UK Government re-affirmed this policy in February 2018.[2]

2. The UK Government was determined to legitimise its retention of nuclear weapons following the 1996 Advisory Opinion of the International Court of Justice (ICJ) that the threat or use of nuclear weapons "*would generally be contrary to the rules of international law*".[3] In 1998, when ratifying Protocol 1 Additional to the 1949 Geneva Conventions ('Additional Protocol 1'), the UK attached a reservation stating that the new rules introduced by the Protocol did not apply to nuclear weapons.[4] Then in February 2017, following a case brought by the Marshall Islands accusing the UK of noncompliance with its disarmament obligation in NPT Article VI reinforced by the 1996 ICJ judgment, the British Government drastically restricted and effectively repudiated the authority of the International Court of Justice on nuclear weapon matters.[5]

3. On 7 July 2017, a Treaty on the Prohibition of Nuclear Weapons (TPNW) was adopted by 122 member states of the UN General Assembly.[6] The treaty's core prohibitions include the threat, let alone use, of nuclear weapons. The nuclear weapon states demonstrated their lack of good faith to comply with NPT Article VI by boycotting the negotiations, and they have refused to sign the TPNW. It will enter into force after 50 states ratify it; at the time of writing, 20 have done so. This is faster than any previous such treaty, and suggests that the fiftieth ratification could occur before the next NPT Review Conference in 2020.

4. Because it incorporates all normative developments outlawing nuclear weapons, the TPNW significantly strengthens the stigmatisation of nuclear deterrence. Yet one *Trident*-armed Royal Navy submarine (SSBN) is being kept on Continuous at Sea Deployment, which the Government asserts is 'essential to assure the invulnerability of the deterrent'. Unstated is the need to sustain the option of re-targeting and operational efficiency. In practice, such escalation would require the SSBN Commanding Officer to decide if the Prime Minister's order to fire was lawful, which would entail being informed of the target(s). Without this, he and his command team – who, unlike the Prime Minister, carry the huge responsibility of being required to carry out such an order – could be placed in legal jeopardy.

5. Additionally, the Rome Statute of 1998 (which entered into force in

2002) confirmed that causing excessive incidental death, injury or damage is a war crime.[7] This means that any re-targeting which is liable to cause excessive incidental death... etc to civilian populations would be within the jurisdiction of the International Criminal Court and, since that is not a new rule of International Law, is out-with the legal sidesteps the UK took regarding Additional Protocol 1 (cf.para 2) which it re-iterated on ratifying the Rome Statute. Such re-targeting would constitute a crime under the International Criminal Court Act 2001.

The Chilcot Report

6. When the decision to de-target missiles was made in 1994 this set in motion – almost certainly unintentionally – a potential pathway to disarmament. The actual intent was to follow the US and Russian lead, as described earlier. At that time the Government would have assumed that it could re-target at any time at its discretion. However, Sir John Chilcot's Inquiry report into the circumstances surrounding Britain's involvement in the 2003 invasion of Iraq included several significant recommendations relevant to any future decision to go to war. The following extracts from a recent report by the Public Accounts and Constitutional Affairs Committee[8] clearly establish the need for Parliament's involvement in the process:

58. The Iraq Inquiry reported that the Blair Government did not expose key policy decisions to rigorous review. The failure to open up key decisions to sufficient, high-level challenge is drawn out by Sir John Chilcot in his statement at the launch of the report: "Above all, the lesson is that all aspects of any intervention need to be calculated, debated and challenged with the utmost rigour."

60. The absence of robust challenge within Government gains particular significance when considering how the legal advice underpinning the Government's case for war was presented and discussed within Cabinet ...

70. Sir John Chilcot said that he believed there was room for Parliament, "whether on the Floor of the Chamber, in Select Committees or in other respects, to exert more influence on Government and to hold Government more effectively to account."

71. We believe that the ongoing issue of Parliament's access to sensitive information underpins the need for an open conversation between Government and Parliament on this matter, so that Parliament can be confident of its full ability to scrutinise Government decisions.

79. We, as Parliamentarians, must also reflect upon how Parliament could have been more critical and challenging of the Government at the time. This, we believe, is a vital consideration, not just for the Intelligence and Security Committee, the Foreign Affairs Committee and the Defence Committee but for every Committee of this House. It is a lesson of which we must be consistently mindful, throughout all aspects of our work and scrutiny of Government.

7. These extraordinarily strong recommendations should especially apply to nuclear weapon re-targeting. At this point the potential use of nuclear weapons would become stark reality, requiring rigorous assessment against criteria commonly accepted for a 'Just War', including:

- All other ways of resolving the problem should have been exhausted first.
- The means used must be in proportion to the desired end result.
- Innocent people and non-combatants should not be harmed.
- Only appropriate and sufficient force to achieve the aim should be used.
- Internationally agreed conventions regulating war must be obeyed.

8. As the ICJ observed in 1996, the destructive power of nuclear weapons cannot be contained in space or time. The reality of the use of nuclear weapons – which, by their very nature, are completely disproportionate, incapable of distinguishing between civilians and military, and long-lasting in their effects – makes it inconceivable that any Parliamentary involvement would approve re-targeting requiring, as it does, specific knowledge of the targets and thereby appreciation of the potential to kill unimaginable numbers of civilians. Such a process is especially important for the deployed *Trident* submarine command team, who have to decide whether to carry out the firing order.

Conclusion

9. Recent developments have strengthened the legal norms stigmatising nuclear deterrence. This means that, despite attempts by the UK Government to bypass them, the process of nuclear weapon retargeting could expose both the Prime Minister and the SSBN Commanding Officer to legal and moral jeopardy. The logic of this argument post-Chilcot is so compelling that the process of nuclear weapon re-targeting, together with its legal implications, needs to be subject to Parliamentary approval in an appropriate manner.

Acknowledgments: Professor Nick Grief, BA PhD SFHEA, Commander Rob Green RN (Ret'd) and Mr Mike Kiely have all contributed to this article.

References

1. Ian Davis, The British Bomb and NATO (SIPRI, 2015), pp18-19: http://www.nucleareducationtrust.org/sites/default/files/NATO%20Trident%20Repo rt%2015_11.pdf
2. HMG Paper 'The UK's nuclear deterrent: what you need to know', 19 February 2018: https://www.gov.uk/government/publications/uk-nuclear-deterrence-factsheet/uk-nuclear-deterrencewhat- you-need-to-know
3. ICJ Advisory Opinion on the Threat or Use of Nuclear Weapons, 8 July 1996, p266: https://www.icj-cij.org/files/case-related/95/095-19960708-ADV-01-00-EN.pdf
4. UK Reservation on ratifying AP1 to Geneva Conventions: https://ihldatabases.icrc.org/ihl/NORM/0A9E03F0F2EE757CC1256402003FB6D2 ?OpenDocument
5. Amended UK declaration regarding acceptance of ICJ compulsory jurisdiction, 22 February 2017: https://www.icj-cij.org/en/declarations/gb 6. Treaty on the Prohibition of Nuclear Weapons, 7 July 2017: http://www.icanw.org/wp-content/uploads/2017/07/TPNW-English1.pdf
7. Article 8 (2) (b) (iv) of the Rome Statute https://www.icc-cpi.int/nr/rdonlyres/ea9aeff7-5752-4f84-be940a655eb30e16/0/rome_ statute_english.pdf
8. Public Accounts and Constitutional Affairs Committee (PACAC), 'Lessons still to be learned from the Chilcot Inquiry', 17 March 2017: https://publications.parliament.uk/pa/cm201617/cmselect/cmpubadm/656/656.pdf

Trident SSBN Commanding Officers
Discharge of Responsibility
Need for re-assurance that Parliament has been involved

A Supplement to 'Re-Targetting Trident – Parliament should be involved'

Introduction

1. The referenced paper and this supplement to it have both been written in the light of my personal experiences as a former nuclear submarine Commanding Officer (CO) at sea in the 1970s when the Cold War was at its height. This included two years as Executive Officer (and in Command for part of one patrol) of *HMS Repulse*, a *Polaris* missile equipped submarine. During this period UK policy was very straightforward; if the Soviets launched an attack on the West with nuclear weapons we would retaliate by firing our *Polaris* missiles – known as Second Strike or, more popularly, Mutually Assured Destruction (MAD).

2. US policy was also stated publicly to be Second Strike. However, Daniel Ellsberg in his 2017 book *The Doomsday Machine: Confessions of a Nuclear War Planner*, stated that the actual plan was to launch a massive pre-emptive First Strike on military complexes and centres of population in the Soviet Union and China together at the first sign of any form of hostile action against the West – even if nuclear weapons were not involved. The intention was to destroy infrastructure and populations so completely that neither State could launch their own First Strike. Furthermore, Ellsberg reveals a frightening lack of control of local commanders of nuclear weapon forces, such that it was entirely possible they might order an attack on their own initiative, so heightening the prospect of launch on a false warning similar to the recent one in Hawaii.

3. While the control of RN *Polaris* was nowhere near as lax as the US seems to have been, had the US initiated a First Strike it is almost certain that the UK would have joined with them; thereby undermining my understanding at the time that the UK *Polaris* would only be used as a Second Strike. This has made me realise that the horrifically disproportionate and indiscriminate nature of nuclear

weapons must involve Parliament because *Trident* is a political not a military weapon.[1] By agreeing overall policy for its use and approving its re-targeting and use (as discussed in the reference paper) against a hostile State, this would be critical to the COs of *Trident* SSBNs who have to decide if they can rightfully obey a launch order. The factors affecting a Commanding Officer making such a decision are now discussed in more detail.

Responsibilities of Trident SSBN Commanding Officers if ordered to launch missiles

4. *The Joint Services Manual of The Law of Armed Conflict* - JSP 383 (2004) provides advice to military commanders which includes *Trident* SSBN COs. The circumstances in which they might be ordered to fire are immeasurably more complex than in my day. Since the Cold War ended, international law governing the threat or use of nuclear weapons has become much more, if not totally, restrictive. Yet, at the same time, the UK Government has broadened its policy from the single circumstance leading to a Second Strike to a much more complex set of circumstances encompassing 'sub-strategic response'. This envisages, for instance, a First Strike using 'low yield' nuclear warheads in support of troops in the field when nuclear weapons have not yet been used – or even possible use of a 'very low yield warning shot' to demonstrate resolve. These options seriously challenge the claim that *Trident* is a 'Weapon of Last Resort'. While the effects might be relatively limited compared to those of a standard 100 kiloton *Trident* warhead, the implications would be so complex and serious that an SSBN CO at sea on patrol could not be expected to assess them. Knowing that Parliament supports the order to launch, this might provide him with some re-assurance in deciding how to use his discretion in discharging his responsibility. The relevant extracts from JSP 383 defining his actions are reproduced below.

Level of responsibility
Paragraph 5.32.9
'The level at which the legal responsibility to take precautions in attack rests is not specified in Additional Protocol I.[2] Those who plan or decide upon attacks are the planners and commanders and they have a duty to verify targets, take precautions to reduce incidental damage, and refrain from attacks that offend the proportionality principle. Whether a person

will have this responsibility will depend on whether he has any discretion in the way the attack is carried out and so the responsibility will range from commanders-in-chief and their planning staff to single soldiers opening fire on their own initiative. Those who do not have this discretion but merely carry out orders for an attack also have a responsibility: to cancel or suspend the attack if it turns out that the object to be attacked is going to be such that the proportionality rule would be breached.'[3]

Assessing discharge of responsibility
Paragraph 5.32.10

'In considering whether commanders and others responsible for planning, deciding upon, or executing attacks have fulfilled their responsibilities, it must be borne in mind that they have to make their decisions on the basis of their assessment of the information from all sources which is available to them at the relevant time. This means looking at the situation as it appeared to the individual at the time when he made his decision. The obligation to cancel or suspend attacks only extends to those who have the authority and the practical possibility to do so as laid down in national laws, regulations, or instructions or agreed rules for NATO or other joint operations.'

5. From Paragraph 5.32.10 one can see that, in order to discharge his responsibilities, an SSBN CO will therefore need sufficient information to be satisfied that the effects of the attack will be consistent with the fundamental principles of humanitarian law as set out, in particular, in Part IV of Additional Protocol 1 (Civilian population); bearing in mind that the principle of proportionality 'cannot … destroy the structure of the system, nor cast doubt upon the fundamental principles of humanitarian law…' Thus an attack cannot be justified only on grounds of proportionality if it contravenes the above-mentioned principles.[4]

6. In simple terms, the CO cannot just fire 'blind' solely because the order has been verified as emanating from the Prime Minister; to do this could place him in legal and moral jeopardy both by JSP 383 and under ICC Article 33 as it relates to individual responsibility for war crimes.[5] At the very least he would need to know:

- justification for firing
- the target(s) and the likely effect of the selected warheads

• that the Attorney General had categorically stated that the firing would be legal under International Law

7. However, bearing in mind the extreme devastation that a nuclear weapon will cause – they were, after all, designed specifically to kill very large numbers of a population indiscriminately under the policy of MAD – the CO will additionally need to know that Parliament has been involved in the political decision to target a hostile State and subsequently launch nuclear weapon(s).

8. The so called 'letter of last resort' should be treated in a similar manner. At present it is a private communication between the Prime Minister and SSBN COs. It is entirely consistent and reasonable to say that its contents, although almost certainly related to extreme existential circumstances, should be approved by Parliament in an appropriate manner.

References

1. ' …the UK views its nuclear weapons as political not military weapons.' Extract from letter to Commander Forsyth from Director General Nuclear Secretariat, 12 February 2018.

2. Protocol 1 Additional to the Geneva Conventions of 1949 (AP1) and Relating to the Protection of Victims of International Armed Conflicts 1977. An HMG Reservation attached to it states that this protocol does not apply to nuclear weapons. As the Protocol does not discuss types of weapons, only the effects to be avoided, the basis for this statement is unclear.

3. The CO has this responsibility and has the discretion to cancel or suspend attacks.

4. ICRC Commentary on Article 57 of AP1, Precautions in attack, para 2207.

5. Nuremberg Principle IV relates to superior orders and command responsibility and states: 'The fact that a person acted pursuant to order of his Government or of a superior does not relieve him from responsibility under international law, provided a moral choice was in fact possible to him.'

CHAPTER IV

Correspondence between Commander Robert Forsyth RN (Ret'd) and the Ministry of Defence (Nuclear Policy)

November 2017 – November 2018

Preamble

This exchange of letters and emails was prompted by my personal concern as to whether the Commanding Officer (CO) of a *Trident* submarine could be placed in legal and moral jeopardy should they be called upon to fire. I thought it appropriate to write in the first instance to Rear Admiral Submarines who heads up the submarine service. He obviously felt it was not appropriate for himself to reply because he passed my letter to MoD/Nuclear Policy. It is perhaps a sign of just how closely controlled nuclear matters are by that department that he felt unable to advise me that this was what he was required to do. It also struck me as somewhat 'Orwellian' that, when the MoD responded, it did so anonymously.

Essentially, I was asking questions that I would want answers to if I was a new CO prior to going on patrol. As MoD accepts (para 4 of Document 2), the legality of a decision to fire nuclear weapons depends on a very wide range of factors which a CO has to consider. As a military commander, they would turn to the advice contained in the *Manual on the Law of Armed Conflict* (JSP 383) which specifically requires them to verify targets and observe the rules of proportionality for the protection of civilians as contained in Additional Protocol 1 (AP1) to the Geneva Conventions. This means it is not sufficient for the CO solely to authenticate that the Prime Minister has authorised the order. They must personally weigh the consequences in the light of existing International Law.

In the correspondence that followed, the MoD consistently repeated that Government policy complies with International Law. Eventually, when pressed on the accuracy of the advice provided in JSP 383 (Document 8), it provided an explanation as to why the JSP explicitly states that AP1 only applies to conventional and not to nuclear weapons. MoD said the reason is that the use of nuclear weapons was not specifically discussed at the diplomatic conference that adopted AP1 in 1977. It is correct that the conference left discussion on which weapons might break the rules to other international legal and jurisdiction bodies and focused entirely on the rules. This explanation is not contained in JSP 383 and so military commanders would reasonably deduce that it was a specific conclusion of the conference that nuclear weapons would not breach the rules rather than the UK (and four other States) asserting an opinion which was not shared by the 169 other States party to AP1.

At the end of the correspondence any doubts I might have had as to whether my concerns were justified had increased. The fact that HMG has spent so much effort on artificially seeking quasi-legal loopholes to justify its nuclear weapons policy gives rise to fundamental questions about the ethics and legality of that policy. More worryingly, it confirms that our *Trident* submarine COs are not being provided with accurate legal facts with which to form their own ethical and legal judgements.

Documents following:

From Commander R Forsyth RN

Rear Admiral J Weale OBE RN
Rear Admiral Submarines
Northwood Headquarters
Sandy Lane
Northwood
Middlesex
HA6 3HP
28 December 2017

1.   You may be aware from tribal gossip and my article in *The Naval Review* (Feb '16) and subsequent letters that I have been questioning the value of Trident in the light of the present parlous state of the RN and the absence of any present or realistically foreseeable threat requiring the use of the Trident weapons system and, in particular, Government statements about willingness to conduct pre-emptive First Strikes. My concerns are such that I feel I must express them directly to yourself and would welcome your response by discussion or letter as you wish. I will try to be brief but I have realised that the subject of Trident is not a simple one easily discussed in sound bites as it too often is in the media and by the Government

2.   Post leaving the service and whilst healthy budget environments generally prevailed I continued to subscribe to my serving day's view as to whether we should have nuclear weapons? The answer being No of course in an ideal world - but I accepted the concept of deterrence so long as the Soviets threatened world peace. I was encouraged that the UK was committed by the **Non-Proliferation Treaty** (NPT) of 1968 to reducing - and hopefully eliminating completely - nuclear weapons. The UK decision, following *Glasnost*, to reduce the onboard load to 8 missiles and 40 warheads seemed to me to be a good start.

3.   However, as budget have been cut again and again, our ASW capability above, on and under the water has declined to the point of being not quite meaningless but certainly well below the level of defence an island nation dependent on sea trade deserves and needs. I have in the last year or so taken the matter very much more seriously. Would you expect an ex Teacher to do anything less? My conclusion is that today Trident does not keep us safe as the Government avers, but, quite the contrary, makes us significantly less safe by becoming perilously close to being a weapon of near first resort rather than one of very last resort at the end of a long chain of political and military options. But I hear a lot of very dangerous talk of it now being used as a First Strike against rogue states. Both Geoffrey Hoon as Secretary of State as long ago as 20 March 2002 stated this and, more recently, on 18 July last year in

Parliament, the Prime Minister publicly supported the concept of First Strike thereby bringing Trident into play as a military weapon rather than the political one of deterrence for which it was originally intend

.

4.   This alarmed me and I so I explored the implications of First Strike. Militarily I could not find any circumstance in which we would intentionally launch even a single nuclear war head deliberately at a rogue state. It would have such enormous political, humanitarian and geo-physical repercussions as to be completely self defeating and, in any case, deny anyone the opportunity to occupy the ground afterwards. However, on paper, First Strike is now a UK military option and one that Trident CO's may therefore be required to respond to. Having now researched the development of International Humanitarian Law since my time in service on the issue of use of nuclear weapons this has caused me to fear for the legal position that *Vanguard* COs (and *Dreadnought* COs idc) may be placed in.

5.   In 1972, when I was Executive Officer of *Repulse (Stbd)* and prior to going on our first patrol, my CO (Tom Green now deceased) and I discussed the legality of accepting an order to fire observing that the **Nuremberg Charter Principle 3** states: '*The fact that a person who committed an act which constitutes a crime under international law acted as Head of State or responsible government official does not relieve him from responsibility under international law.*' We wished to be clear that we were both were of the same thinking; not only was I a key member of the firing chain but I would assume command should he be out of action - as indeed occurred for medical reasons on one patrol.

6.   We well understood that **The Geneva Conventions** require that the methods and means used in military actions 'must be proportionate to the military objective and that tactics or the excessive use of force that cause unnecessary death or destruction among civilians is prohibited'. The indiscriminate nature of nuclear weapons - and UK Polaris ones in particular - was such that, although they could be accurately targeted on military installations, we were well aware that the subsequent blast and radiation effects could kill thousands, if not millions, of civilians because the Soviets located military installations near heavily populated areas. Furthermore the radiation would continue to be dispersed over considerable distances by wind direction and force.

7.   However, we were absolutely confident that we would only be ordered to fire should a Soviet nuclear attack already be in progress (Second Strike). Whilst any such response meant that the policy of deterrence had failed and it might be a futile gesture, the circumstances would so far transcend any normal warfare - the physical survival of the UK and Europe and more might well be at stake - that we were agreed that we could and would obey such an order. Several of our contemporaries were unable to reach the same conclusion and declined to serve in SSBN's.

8.   Nonetheless, in order to confirm that we would only be responding to an attack in progress, we agreed that were we to receive an order to fire with no corroborating indication to support this then we would hold the firing sequence while we examined and discussed the situation. Monitoring the BBC 24 hours a day was an important aspect of this. We were not alone in this and, interestingly, Lord Peter Hennessy refers to it in his book *The Silent Deep*. The corollary was that we were prepared not to fire unless it was assuredly as a Second Strike.

9.   A more recent affirmation of the need to be sure of the legality of an order to fire was a statement by the current CINC US Strategic Command, General John Hyten USAF. In answer to a question about receiving an illegal order from the President to launch nuclear weapons, he responded "If you execute an unlawful order, you will go to jail. You could go to jail for the rest of your life." *(The Guardian 19.11.2017)*. General Hyten was clearly speaking on behalf of his military subordinates who would execute the order. In so doing, he acknowledged that there were scenarios where launching nuclear weapons would be unlawful.

10.   The problem here lies in how to satisfy the officers with responsibility for obeying that command that the order is legal. If the CINC has a responsibility to question it's legality then so do his subordinates - including the COs at sea.

11.   My research shows that pre-emptive (First Strike) use of nuclear weapons is now clearly stated to be illegal by the international community via:
> a.   **Protocol 1 to The Geneva Conventions** (8 June 1977)
> b.   an **International Court of Justice** ruling (8 July 1996)
> c.   **Rome Statute of the International Criminal Court** (17 July 1998).
> d.   In July 2017, 122 of the 186 countries not in possession of nuclear weapons went even further and adopted a **Treaty on the Prohibition of Nuclear Weapons** banning not only the use but also the threat of their use completely, thereby bringing nuclear weapons in line with other chemical and biological weapons banned since 1925.

12.   The UK Government has sought to ascribe legality to nuclear weapons by a variety of means including:
> (a) appending a **Reservation to the Geneva Conventions** stating: *'It continues to be the understanding of the United Kingdom that the rules introduced by the Protocol (1) apply exclusively to conventional weapons ...In particular, the rules so introduced do not have any effect on and do not regulate or prohibit the use of nuclear weapons'*
> (b) not signing the recent **UN Nuclear Weapon Ban Treaty.**

Such actions may satisfy the Attorney General's view of legality but the 122 nations party to the UN ban and its previous IHL treaties and laws will not, particularly if used as a First Strike.

13.   I am therefore very concerned as to how much consideration today's Fleet Commanders, *Vanguard* COs and their command teams have given to this and whether they appreciate the legal jeopardy they will be in if ordered to launch a Trident missile attack. I would be interested to know how you and they reconcile International Humanitarian Law with an order from the Prime Minister which the rest of the world outside of the nuclear powers will consider to be illegal and from which there will be no defence of obeying superior orders under the terms of **The Nuremberg Charter.**

Ministry
of Defence

Ministry of Defence
Main Building
Whitehall
London SW1A 2HB
United Kingdom

Telephone: +44 (0)20 7218 9000
Email:
DGNuc-Secretariat-Parliamentary@mod.gov.u

Commander (Rtd) Robert Forsyth

Our Reference: TO2018/02132

Date: 12 February 2018

Dear Cdr Forsyth,

Thank you for your letter dated 28 December addressed to Rear Admiral Weale, Assistant Chief of Naval Staff Submarines, regarding the Nuclear Non Proliferation Treaty (NPT) and the United Kingdom's (UK) nuclear posture. As my department is responsible for the policy on this important matter, I have been asked to respond on behalf of Rear Admiral Weale.

As I am sure you will appreciate, we cannot un-invent nuclear weapons. Indeed, we have to acknowledge that nuclear weapons have undoubtedly contributed to global security and stability since the end of World War II. Nevertheless, the UK looks forward to a nuclear weapon free world, when all nuclear-armed states feel able to relinquish them.

The purpose of the UK's nuclear weapons is to deter and prevent nuclear blackmail and acts of aggression against our vital interests that cannot be countered by other means. I should emphasise, the UK views its nuclear weapons as political not military weapons – their purpose is to deter aggression (a political role), rather than to be used on the battlefield to gain (military) advantage. It is essential, however, that we don't define precisely when, how and at what scale we would contemplate employing them, otherwise we make it easier for our adversaries. Deterrence works and to underpin that I can confirm the UK has neither a first use nor a no first use policy. Essentially, if you believe that the nuclear deterrent is our ultimate security guarantee, then you must accept there are circumstances in which its use would be justified. To give any other answer undermines the credibility of our deterrent and our national security.

The Government agrees with you that the use of nuclear weapons – like all weapons – would be subject to the requirements of international humanitarian law. The UK would not use any of our weapons, whether conventional or nuclear, contrary to international law. Our nuclear deterrent is fully compliant and compatible with our international treaty and legal obligations. The 1996 International Court of Justice Advisory Opinion did not conclude that the threat or use of nuclear weapons would be necessarily unlawful in an extreme circumstance of self-defence in which a State's very survival would be at stake. The International Court of Justice concluded that legality can only be determined in the light of the specific circumstances applying when such use is being contemplated and the application of the general rules of international law, including those regulating the use of force and the conduct of hostilities. We would only consider using our nuclear weapons in the most extreme circumstances of self-defence, including the defence of our NATO allies.

As you acknowledge we have a good record on disarmament. The UK has in fact been a leading nation, having unilaterally reduced our nuclear forces by over half from their Cold War peak in the late 1970s. We are also the only nuclear weapon State recognised under the NPT to have reduced its deterrent capability to a single nuclear weapon system. In addition to dismantling our maritime tactical nuclear capability and the WE177 free fall bomb, and the reductions that you mention to missiles and warheads on board patrols, we have achieved our commitment to reduce the number of operationally available warheads to no more than 120. The UK also remains committed to reducing our overall nuclear weapon stockpile to no more than 180 warheads by the mid-2020s as set out in the 2010 Strategy and Strategic Defence and Security Review. The UK now possesses approximately 1% of the total global stockpile of nuclear weapons, the smallest of all the NPT nuclear weapon States. It is unfortunate that our actions have not been followed by other States and we have not yet been able to create the conditions where nuclear weapons are no longer necessary to guarantee our security. We are now at the minimum level of nuclear capability that is required to credibly deter threats or coercion by nuclear-armed States. To reduce our capability further would undermine UK security and that of our NATO allies.

Nevertheless, the UK Government continues to work with partners across the international community to prevent proliferation and to make progress on multilateral nuclear disarmament. Trust and confidence need to be built between states for tangible steps to be taken towards a safer and more stable world in which countries with nuclear weapons feel able to relinquish them. We, along with our NATO allies, do not believe that the treaty prohibiting nuclear weapons (or Ban Treaty) will bring us closer to this goal. A ban on nuclear weapons will not in itself improve the international security environment or increase trust and transparency between nuclear weapon possessor states, nor will it address the considerable technical and procedural challenges involved in nuclear disarmament verification. The NPT is the cornerstone of the global non-proliferation and disarmament regime. A ban treaty would shift focus from the step-by-step approach on disarmament addressed by the NPT, which includes working towards next steps on banning nuclear testing and ending fissile material production – steps the UK has supported to help achieve the goal of a nuclear weapon free world.

I trust that this broad explanation of the UK's extant defence nuclear posture helps with your continued understanding and puts into context the position the Prime Minister took in Parliament during the Nuclear Deterrent debate on 18 July 2016.

Yours sincerely,

Director General Nuclear Secretariat

From: Rob Forsyth [mailto:

Sent: 28 February 2018 13:13

To: DGNuc-Secretariat-Parliamentary (MULTIUSER) <DGNuc-Secretariat-

Parliamentary@mod.gov.uk>

Subject: RE: Reference: Letter your ref: TO2018/02132 dated 12 February 2018

I received the reference letter recently. It has no name of writer or a signature. Please could you
advise the name/position of the sender.

Regards Robert Forsyth

Cdr RN (Ret'd)

From: **DGNuc-Secretariat-Parliamentary (MULTIUSER) <DGNuc-Secretariat-**

Parliamentary@mod.gov.uk>

Sent: 28 February 2018 15:07

To: Rob Forsyth

Cc: DGNuc-Secretariat-Parliamentary (MULTIUSER)

Subject:RE: Reference: Letter your ref: TO2018/02132 dated 12 February 2018

Good afternoon Robert,

Due to the sensitive nature of our work, it is our policy not to release names of individuals below
1* level.

Kind Regards,

Defence Nuclear Organisation Secretariat

From: Commander R Forsyth RN (Ret'd)

Mr Julian Kelly
Director General Nuclear Secretariat
MOD Main Building
London SW1A 2HB

7 March 2018

Dear Mr Kelly

Nuclear Weapons Policy

Your Reference: TO2018/02132 dated 12 February 2018

I am writing in response to the reference which bore no signature or name. I understand that " *Due to the sensitive nature of our work, it is our policy not to release names of individuals below 1* level.* ".

In the first instance, I would have thought that my letter, being from a former Executive Officer of an SSBN, Commanding Officer of two submarines (including an SSN) and Commanding Officer (Teacher) of the Commanding Officer's Qualifying Course (Perisher), deserved a response from at least 1* star level on such a serious subject.

Secondly, for a Government Department to hide behind anonymity comes across as somewhat 'Orwellian' and suggests that no one is prepared to accept responsibility for its contents even though the reference was written in the first person. I consider that the staff of the Nuclear Secretariat should be as publicly accountable by name as any other Government Department.

Your department's reply laid out the Government's position and, in doing so, made some sweeping assumptions. I would like to comment on two of these:

1. The fact that nuclear weapons have never been used since 1945 is no proof of deterrence having worked; it is an opinion. Others have different opinions and would say that it is entirely possible that no nation, aware of the devastating consequences, ever seriously intended to use nuclear weapons but felt driven to keep up with the nuclear arms race.

2. It is a truism to say that you cannot uninvent nuclear weapons; no more can you uninvent chemical and biological weapons or any other form of warfare. You can, however, decide to prohibit them in the same way that chemical and biological weapons have been by international agreements – to which the UK is party. The UN Treaty on the Prohibition of Nuclear Weapons seeks to do just that but the UK has elected not to sign it.

   I note also that the Government added a Reservation to Protocol 1 of the Geneva Conventions when they signed it. The Protocol includes a large number of provisions for the protection of civilians in warfare. The UK Reservation reads in part " *... the rules...do not have any effect on and do not regulate or prohibit the use of nuclear weapons.* " This Reservation was repeated in 1998 and clearly is an attempt to provide legal cover for the use of nuclear weapons while continuing to comply with the ban on the much less lethal chemical and biological weapons.

One Government policy the reference did confirm, however, was that it was prepared to pre-empt an attack employing First Use of nuclear weapons if it ever considered this necessary. The reference clearly states that this option is not ruled out - so by definition it can also be ruled in. The Secretary of State for Defence, in a 2002 BBC interview, also said that the UK was prepared to use nuclear weapons against rogue states such as Iraq if they used "*weapons of mass destruction*" i.e. including non-nuclear ones. This was also implicit in the Prime Minister's answer to a question from the Opposition in the Parliamentary Debate on 18 July 2016 in which she also said that anyone who did not support her view was 'a traitor'. This comment places the CO of an SSBN on patrol in an invidious position faced with a personal decision as to whether an order to fire is legal, observing that blind obedience to a superior's order, even under coercion, is not a defence. One hopes that it was political hyperbole.

In justification of Government policy, and thereby implying SSBN COs would be legally safe, the reference paraphrased the 1996 International Court of Justice's (ICJ) Advisory Opinion, para 96 here quoted in full:

> "*..the court cannot conclude definitively whether the threat or use of nuclear weapons would be lawful or unlawful in an extreme circumstance of self-defence, in which the very survival of a State would be at stake.*"

The logical interpretation of this, as the reference correctly said, is '*that legality can only be determined in the light of the specific circumstances..*' Bearing in mind that the Opinion also says elsewhere:

> '*self-defence... would warrant only measures which are **proportional** to the armed attack*' (My emphasis. Paras 41 & 42)

> "*....In the view of the vast majority of States there can be no doubt as to the applicability of humanitarian law to nuclear weapons...The Court shares that view... In general, international humanitarian law bears on the threat or use of nuclear weapons as it does of other weapons.* " (Paras 85 & 86)

> "*A threat or use of nuclear weapons should also be compatible with the requirements of the international law applicable in armed conflict, particularly those of the principles and rules of international humanitarian law...*" (Paras 105.2d)

...then it is apparent that the full opinion, taken together with the Geneva Conventions and the Rome Statute of the ICC (2002), means that confirming compliance with International Humanitarian Law for any use of nuclear weapons is likely to be unsuccessful. In any case it will be an extremely difficult, complex and time consuming process. The introduction of policies of First use and/or against threats not necessarily from nuclear weapons has made the legal position even more complex, even less likely to be approved and one which an SSBN CO on patrol cannot possibly resolve legally for himself. As I asked in my original letter, how is the CO at sea protected from potential legal jeopardy?

Under these circumstances, should the Government not revert, at the very least, to a policy of No First Use and even then only in response to an attack with nuclear weapons? This would allow the CO to know before sailing what the sole criteria would be for ordering missile launch. He can then make a personal decision as to whether he can accept responsibility to authorise the launch.

Yours sincerely

Ministry of Defence

Ministry of Defence
Main Building
Whitehall
London SW1A 2HB
United Kingdom

Telephone: +44 (0)20 7218 9000
Email: Nuclear-SecretariatTeam@mod.gov.uk

Commander (Rtd) Robert Forsyth

Our Reference:
TO2018/03750

12 April 2018

Dear Commander Forsyth

Thank you for your letter of 7 March to Julian Kelly, Director General Nuclear. I have been asked to respond on his behalf, as I am the head of the Defence Nuclear organisation's secretariat team.

As I am sure you will understand, the Ministry Of Defence receives a high volume of correspondence, particularly regarding the United Kingdom's (UK) nuclear deterrent, and as such it is not possible for each to have a response at One-Star level. Also, in the context of nuclear matters, it is normal practice to not release the names of junior staff hence the reason for no individual's name appearing in the signature block. This information is considered personal information and is protected under the Freedom of Information Act 2000 as well as the Data Protection Act 1998.

I am sorry that you felt that the response from the Department, dated 12 February, fell short of answering the points you made. That was certainly not the intent and I will now endeavour to respond to them. I must, however, first address your assertion that the Prime Minister said in Parliament that anyone who did not support her in the use of nuclear weapons was a "traitor". That is not the case. The Prime Minister was asked if she would authorise a nuclear strike. Hansard records the exchange and the point being made, also highlighted in the letter of 12 February, was that if one believed the nuclear deterrent to be our ultimate security guarantee, as successive governments have, then it must be accepted there are circumstances in which its use would be justified. Therefore, to provide any other answer than that given by the Prime Minister would undermine the credibility of our deterrent and our national security.

I note your view that it is an opinion to suggest that deterrence is working as a nuclear weapon had not been used since 1945. Nevertheless, the UK has long been clear that our independent nuclear deterrent exists to deter the most extreme threats to our national security and way of life, and that of our allies. It has done so for over 60 years and, with the Government's decision to maintain the deterrent, will help guarantee our security into the 2050s and beyond. To be clear we hope never to employ nuclear weapons but to deliver a deterrent effect under all circumstances.

The UK remains committed to creating the conditions for a world without nuclear weapons. However, as previously stated, we do not believe the United Nations treaty on the prohibition of nuclear weapons will bring us closer to this goal. We consider the step by step approach to multilateral nuclear disarmament delivered through the nuclear Non-Proliferation Treaty as the cornerstone of efforts to pursue the goal.

The use of nuclear weapons – like all weapons – would be subject to the requirements of international humanitarian law. Therefore, only the Prime Minister can authorise the firing of these weapons, even if employed as part of a NATO response, and the Commanding Officer of the ballistic missile submarine must confirm the authorisation to fire meets the rigorous confirmation processes in place - these I am sure you will understand I cannot discuss.

Although we keep our nuclear posture under constant review in the light of the international security environment and the actions of potential adversaries, I shall however if I may, reaffirm that the UK has neither a first use nor a no first use policy. I am sure you will understand why it is essential that we would want to avoid making it easier for our adversaries' calculations by defining precisely when, how and at what scale we would contemplate employing nuclear weapons. As previously stated, we judge that our nuclear deterrent is fully compliant and compatible with our international treaty and legal obligations - the UK would not use any of its weapons, whether conventional or nuclear, contrary to international law.

Yours sincerely,

Mark Newman
Defence Nuclear Secretariat

Rob Forsyth

From: Rob Forsyth ·
Sent: 12 April 2018 16:20
To: 'Nuclear-Secretariat Team (MULTIUSER)'
Subject: RE: 20180326_Forsyth-Nuclear Weapons_Legality

Dear Mr Newman

I will, if I may respond, but realistically do not expect you to respond back.

1. The PM definitely used the word Traitor because I was watching the debate on TV and my wife recalls me storming out of the room in anger. Why it is not recorded in Hansard I know not although I have been told that it is not necessarily 100% verbatim.

2. A policy of not saying whether First Use is IN or OUT means that it can be IN. It is specious to try and say otherwise. There is world of moral and legal difference between the two and I note that there is a large body of opinion among those who do support Deterrence to say that this does not require First Use as part of the policy. It is immoral, unethical and illegal.

3. You say that UK meets all International and Treaty obligations - but I consider that this is only because UK has placed a Reservation on the Geneva Conventions and, I now find post my letter of 7 April, that last ye UK amended its Declaration of Consent to ICJ's Authority to say (inter alia) that UK will only recognise it if 5 NPT states are simultaneously involved with respect to nuclear weapons and disarmament. The chance of this happening, of course, are near zero; so UK has effectively withdrawn from ICJ's Authority and compliance with Geneva Conventions on any nuclear or disarmament matter?

4. With respect to the point about the Commanding Officer - you have completely missed my point. I am qu sure today's COs follow the correct procedures to verify the authority of an order to fire - I did so myself f many WSRTs in 1974/75. However, the CO has a _personal_ responsibility under Nuremberg Charter and Military Law to satisfy himself that the authenticated order is in itself a lawful order. The fact that it emanates from the PM (or her authorised deputy) does not absolve him from this. There are many documented cases of war crimes conducted by a junior in response to a senior's order in which obedience a superior was not a defence. The Commanding Officer therefore has to take reasonable steps to assure himself of his position. I am merely pointing out that an increasingly complex military, political and legal scenario has developed since I was faced with the single simple question " Can I legally respond to an orde to fire (second strike) in response to a massive nuclear attack underway from Soviet Russia" . This has complicated today's CO's position such that I cannot see how he can resolve it at sea on patrol.

I therefore stand by my opinions and continue to be concerned at HMG policy. Sir Michael Quinlan, who was the codifier of UK Nuclear policy and supported UK compliance with the policy of M.A.D. would also be concerned I a sure.

Yours sincerely

Robert Forsyth

From: "Rob Forsyth"

Date: 11 September 2018 at 14:54:02 BST

To: "'Nuclear-Secretariat Team \(MULTIUSER\)'" <Nuclear-SecretariatTeam@mod.gov.uk>

Subject: RE: Parliamentary Question by Caroline Lucas MP

Dear Sir

Reference the following Q & A :

> Question by Caroline Lucas Co-Leader of the Green Party
>
> To ask the Secretary of State for Defence, what assessment he has made of the effect of the 1998 Reservation on Protocol 1 (1977) to the Geneva Conventions on the Government's policy that Trident is compliant with International and Humanitarian Law; and if he will make a statement.
>
> And Reply by Gavin Williamson The Secretary of State for Defence
>
> The position of the United Kingdom remains that the rules introduced by the Protocol apply exclusively to conventional weapons without prejudice to any other rules of international law applicable to other types of weapons. In particular, the rules so introduced do not have any effect on and do not regulate or prohibit the use of nuclear weapons."

I would be interested to know on what grounds does UK consider that the rules do not apply to nuclear weapons. I can find no such reference to this in AP1 so presume this is a legal opinion; if so, how is it derived?

Yours faithfully

Robert Forsyth

Commander RN (Ret'd)

Ministry
of Defence

Ministry of Defence
Main Building
Whitehall
London SW1A 2HB
United Kingdom

Our Ref: TO2018/11838

Your Ref:

Telephone:	+44(0)20 7218 9000
E-mail:	Nuclear-
	SecretariatTeam@mod.gov.uk

Commander (Rtd) Forsyth

3 October 2018

Dear Commander Forsyth,

Thank you for your email dated 11 September 2018, relating to the Parliamentary Question asked by Caroline Lucas MP about the 1998 Reservation on Protocol 1 to the Geneva Conventions, which was answered by the Secretary of State for Defence on 10 September 2018.

Protocol 1 Additional to the four 1949 Geneva Conventions was adopted in 1977 and was ratified by the United Kingdom in 1998. In a letter to the Swiss Government, as the depository of Protocol 1 for ratification, the UK outlined a number of reservations in respect of the ratification by the UK of that Protocol. The first of these reservations was as follows, and you will note that the text is almost exactly the same as that in the Secretary of State's answer to Caroline Lucas's question:

> *"It continues to be the understanding of the United Kingdom that the rules introduced by the Protocol apply exclusively to conventional weapons without prejudice to any other rules of international law applicable to other types of weapons. In particular, the rules so introduced do not have any effect on and do not regulate or prohibit the use of nuclear weapons."*

The Diplomatic Conference on the Development of Humanitarian Law, 1974-1977, which adopted Protocol 1 to the Geneva Conventions of 1949 did not discuss the legality of nuclear weapons. In submitting the draft Protocol 1 (and Protocol 2) to the Diplomatic Conference, the International Committee of the Red Cross (ICRC) stated:

> *"Problems relating to atomic, bacteriological and chemical warfare are subjects of international agreements or negotiations by governments, and in submitting these draft Additional Protocols the ICRC does not intend to broach those problems."*

During the four sessions of the Diplomatic Conference, the UK and a number of other States (including some which are non-nuclear weapons States) made statements to the effect that the subject of nuclear weapons should not be discussed by the Conference. A number of other States made clear that they shared the view of the ICRC that nuclear weapons were best dealt with in the context of disarmament negotiations and that the Conference should do nothing to prejudice such negotiations. Some States did maintain that the Conference should consider a ban on some or all uses of nuclear weapons, but the records of the Conference show that this was not done. Discussion of specific weapons was limited to certain conventional weapons.

You will appreciate that, as nuclear weapons were excluded from discussions during the Diplomatic Conference which adopted Protocol 1, the UK considers that Protocol 1 does not apply to nuclear weapons, and ratified Protocol 1 in 1977 with a reservation to that effect.

Yours sincerely,

Defence Nuclear Organisation Secretariat

From: Commander R Forsyth RN (Ret'd)

Defence Nuclear Organisation Secretariat
MOD Main Building
London SW1A 2HB

8 October 2018

Sir

Thank you for your letter of 3 October 2018 received by email.

Your explanation of the UK's position with regard to the Reservation attached to Additional Protocol 1 (AP1) confirmed that nothing contained within AP1 specifically states that nuclear weapons – or weapons of any sort for that matter – might comply or not with the rules introduced by this Protocol.

The UK's Reservation is no more than an 'Assertion of Opinion'. The fact that the effects of specific weapons were not discussed does not lead to a conclusion that '...*the rules introduced by the Protocol apply exclusively to conventional weapons...*' or to the follow on statement that '*the rules so introduced do not regulate or prohibit the use of nuclear weapons*'. The use of any weapon which failed to comply with the fundamental rules of non-discrimination and proportionality would be in breach of the Protocol.

My concern throughout the whole of my correspondence with your Department has always been 'how does the SSBN Commanding Officer (CO) at sea decide if an order to fire first is lawful[1]?' Firing first invokes a whole complexity of decision making not incurred by the second strike policy of 'if you fire nuclear weapons at us then we will fire back' that prevailed when I was second in command (and temporarily in command) of an SSBN.

I have therefore closely examined the one source that a CO will certainly look to for guidance, namely *JSP 383 THE JOINT SERVICE MANUAL OF THE LAW OF ARMED CONFLICT (2004)*. Two extracts are particularly relevant to my concerns:

> **Responsibility** - extract para 5.32.9
> 'Commanders...have a duty to verify targets, take precautions to reduce incidental damage, and refrain from attacks that offend the proportionality principle.'

So a CO will need at least to know the targets, war yields and an assessment of the likely effects - including blast, heat and radiation - on civilian populations. And, of course, he will need to know the reason for firing. As nuclear weapons are inherently indiscriminate, he will also look for guidance in the section on Nuclear Weapons where para 6.17 is particularly relevant.

---

[1] 'The UK has neither a first use nor a no first use policy' (Mr Newman's letter of 12 April 2018) so firing first is an option.

> **6.17** There is no specific rule of international law, express or implied, which
> prohibits the use of nuclear weapons.[2] The legality of their use depends
> upon the application of the general rules of international law, including
> those regulating the use of force and the conduct of hostilities. Those
> rules cannot be applied in isolation from any factual context to imply a prohibition
> of a general nature. Whether the use, or threatened use, of nuclear
> weapons in a particular case is lawful depends on all the circumstances.
> Nuclear weapons fall to be dealt with by reference to the same general
> principles as apply to other weapons. However, the rules introduced by
> Additional Protocol I apply exclusively to conventional weapons without
> prejudice to any other rules of international law applicable to other types of
> weapons. In particular, the rules so introduced do not have any effect on
> and do not regulate or prohibit the use of nuclear weapons.
> (my emphasis)

Any hesitancy he might feel would be dispelled by the ultimate sentence of para 6.17 which
selectively quotes the UK's Reservation attached to AP1 with no caveat that this is an 'assertion' or
'opinion' or 'understanding'. It is written as fact. Furthermore, the use of the word 'However' at
sentence start would lead him to think that, despite the more cautionary preceding sentences, there
are no constraints on the use of nuclear weapons at all in the case of the rules to be found in AP1.
This not only contradicts the preceding articles but is seriously misleading in the context in which it is
presented.[3]

If the words I have emphasised were to be removed, then the remainder of the preceding paragraph
would be a more accurate representation of the nuclear weapon situation with respect to
International Law. As it stands, SSBN COs who followed its advice would be placed in a position of
legal jeopardy in view of the principle of individual criminal responsibility.

I therefore urge your Department to amend JSP 383 in the way I have suggested in order not to
mislead Commanding Officers on the factors affecting the use of nuclear weapons.

Yours faithfully

Robert Forsyth

---

[2] This is technically correct as it stands today. However, when the UN Treaty on Prohibition of Nuclear
Weapons enters into force, this will need to be amended. Ratification by 50 signatories is required; to date 69
States have signed and 19 have ratified the Treaty.
[3] It is my understanding that the UK reservation to AP1, even if permissible, would not affect the UK's
obligations under customary international law such as the rule prohibiting indiscriminate attacks.

**Ministry
of Defence**

Ministry of Defence
Main Building
Whitehall
London SW1A 2HB
United Kingdom

Our Ref: TO2018/12701

Your Ref:

| Telephone: | +44(0)20 7218 9000 |
| E-mail: | Nuclear-SecretariatTeam@mod.gov.uk |

Commander (Rtd) Forsyth

7 November 2018

Dear Commander Forsyth,

Thank you for your emails dated 9 and 10 October 2018, relating to our earlier response (Our Ref. TO2018/11838) explaining the United Kingdom's view of Protocol 1 to the Geneva Conventions and how it relates to nuclear weapons.

As you allude to in the letter attached to your emails, there is now a series of correspondence between yourself and the Ministry of Defence relating to your underlying concern that using a nuclear weapon may be unlawful and render the Commanding Officer of the submarine subject to legal proceedings.

I appreciate that you hold very strong opinions on this matter, which differ from the Government's view, and I note your request for the Ministry of Defence to amend the content of Joint Service Publication (JSP) 383: The Joint Service Manual of the Law of Armed Conflict.

I should like to start by emphasising that, as we have stated previously, we hope never to employ nuclear weapons but to deliver a deterrent effect under all circumstances. We would only consider using our nuclear weapons in the most extreme circumstances of self-defence, including the defence of our NATO allies, and that we have neither a 'first use' nor a 'no first use' policy as it is essential that we do not simplify the calculations of our potential adversaries by defining exactly when, how and at what scale we would contemplate the use of our nuclear weapons.

The Government is clear that the use of nuclear weapons - like all weapons - would be subject to the requirements of international humanitarian law. As we have previously stated, the 1996 International Court of Justice Advisory Opinion could not reach a definitive conclusion on the legality or illegality of the use of nuclear weapons by a state in an extreme circumstance of self-defence, in which its very survival would be at stake. Legality could only be determined in light of the specific circumstances applying when such use is being contemplated and the application of the general rules of law, particularly those regulating the use of force and the conduct of hostilities. I note your opinion that the United Kingdom's nuclear reservation on our ratification of Protocol 1 Additional to the Geneva Conventions is an "Assertion of Opinion". Nevertheless, for the reasons which we outlined in our letter to you dated 3 October 2018, it continues to be the understanding of the United Kingdom that the rules introduced by the Protocol apply exclusively to conventional weapons without prejudice to any other rules of international law applicable to other types of weapons. In particular, the rules so introduced do not have any effect on and do not regulate or prohibit the use of nuclear weapons. As this continues to be the Government's view, it would not be appropriate to remove this section of the text from JSP 383 as you have requested.

Should the circumstances arise in which use of nuclear weapons needs to be considered, legal aspects would be a contributing factor in the decision-making process. Only the Prime Minister can authorise the use of nuclear weapons, even if employed as part of a NATO response. As we have previously stated, the Commanding Officer of the submarine must confirm that the authorisation to fire meets the rigorous authentication processes in place.

I hope that you will understand that, as we have now written to you on several occasions regarding your concern about the legality of nuclear weapons, I feel we have now reached a point where further correspondence on this matter can serve no purposeful outcome.

Yours sincerely,

Defence Nuclear Organisation Secretariat

In conclusion

The papers gathered together in this collection arise from my search for answers to key questions surrounding the UK Government's decision to continue deploying the *Trident* submarine nuclear weapon system into the 2050s and beyond. *Why Trident?* effectively marks the end of a journey from being one of the command team responsible for launching *Polaris* missiles to concluding that the answer to the question posed by the title is that there is no justifiable answer other than national hubris and egotism: a highly dangerous combination that has fuelled 75 years of an arms race that threatens the existence of the world it allegedly protects.

An underlying concern throughout has been to establish whether *Trident* submarine Commanding Officers (COs) can be confident that an order to fire is lawfully and morally justified, bearing in mind the complexity of international humanitarian law, and that they are unable independently to verify compliance with the law once submerged on patrol. This means that they put not just their legal but also their moral trust in the Prime Minister of the day; to which I would respond in time honoured naval signalling tradition "Psalm 146.v3."[1]

The solution, so long as *Trident* remains in service, is for the Government to establish clear and unambiguous rules for the use of nuclear weapons so that COs, prior to sailing, can make individual decisions as to whether they can accept the responsibility of launching their missiles under those rules. I, personally, would not have liked to have on my conscience, after the event, that I had been an unwitting party to a war crime committed by a Prime Minister. Prime Ministers can, and do, make mistakes as just two quotes from the Chilcot Inquiry (2016) into the 2003 Iraq war show:

> "It is now clear that policy on Iraq (to invade)was made on the basis of flawed intelligence and assessments. They were not challenged, and they should have been."

---

1. King James Bible "Do not put your trust in princes, in mortal men, who cannot save."

"The legal basis on which military action was launched was 'far from satisfactory'".

My fervent wish is for the UK to take the lead on the world stage with unilateral nuclear disarmament (c.f. Appendix VI). If this is not to be the case and the *Trident* nuclear weapon system remains in service, then I believe the UK should demonstrate international leadership by adopting a clear policy of 'No First Use' and 'Sole Use' (i.e. solely in retaliation for a nuclear attack on UK/NATO). Furthermore, in no circumstances should the UK be prepared to initiate 'limited' nuclear war-fighting using low-yield warheads as is openly espoused by the US and also, by implication for lack of denial, by the UK.

I hope that *Why Trident?* shines a light on the failures of successive Governments to address the serious issues I have raised in these pages and contributes to a more open, fact-based debate.

Stop Press: The UN Treaty on the Prohibition of Nuclear Weapons will come into force on 22 January 2021. This follows the 50th State (Honduras) ratifying the treaty on 24 October 2020, the 75th anniversary of the founding of the UN.

In a press release U.N. Secretary-General Antonio Guterres commended the 50 states and saluted "the instrumental work" of civil society in facilitating negotiations and pushing for ratification.

The U.N. chief said the treaty's entry into force on 22 January culminates a worldwide movement "to draw attention to the catastrophic humanitarian consequences of any use of nuclear weapons" and "is a tribute to the survivors of nuclear explosions and tests, many of whom advocated for this treaty". He went on to say that the treaty "represents a meaningful commitment towards the total elimination of nuclear weapons, which remains the highest disarmament priority of the United Nations".

Appendices

Appendix I

The Hiroshima and Nagasaki Atom Bombs were not the reasons why Japan surrendered in WWII

Transcript of a live-streamed talk by Cdr Forsyth at Deddington Parish Church, 16 August 2020

75 years ago two atomic bombs were dropped on Hiroshima (Uranium core) and Nagasaki (Plutonium core). No one really knows how many died but conservative estimates say upwards of 200,000. Anyone who has watched the recent series on the Russian nuclear reactor disaster at Chernobyl will have no illusions about the horrific nature of the eventual deaths of those who survived the initial nuclear explosion.

The accepted wisdom has always been that dropping the bombs was justified because it brought an abrupt end to the war and so saved countless allied lives. Historical facts relate a somewhat different story.

Following the surrender of Germany, the Soviet Union declared war on Japan and moved 1.5 million troops to the East to launch an attack through Manchuria.

The Japanese War Council, at a meeting with the Emperor six weeks before Hiroshima, agreed that they had to negotiate with the Americans or suffer invasion and occupation by the Soviets, with the certain 'elimination' of the Japanese ruling class and execution of their God Emperor. This was unthinkable for the Japanese nation. President Truman was shown an intercepted cable from 18 July 1945 which indicated that the Japanese Emperor wanted to negotiate peace.

After the war US Secretary of War, Henry Stimson, acknowledged that "history might find that the United States, by its delay in stating its position (on surrender terms) had prolonged the war".

The Americans did not want Japan occupied by the Soviets either and, crucially for Japan, were prepared to accept continuation of the Emperor as Head of State as a condition of surrender.

When the atomic bombs were dropped on 6 and 9 August on Hiroshima and Nagasaki respectively, the Japanese War Cabinet minutes barely mentioned them. They were engrossed in discussions about the Soviet invasion when the bomb fell on Nagasaki. Apparently, when a messenger ran in and said "Sir, we've lost Nagasaki, it's been destroyed by a new 'special' bomb'", the chairman simply responded "Thank you".*

One has to understand that a city-destroying weapon was not particularly shocking or new to a country that had already suffered fire bombings of more than 60 cities, including a massive attack in March 1945 on Tokyo that matched Hiroshima or Nagasaki by burning to death 100,000 men, women, and children in one night. The Japanese Cabinet were unaware of the radiation effects which would eventually more than double the number killed by the initial blast.

The decision to surrender was made because the Soviets had completed their invasion and occupation of the South Sakhalin and Kurile Islands (which remain in Russian hands), and were poised to invade mainland Japan.

This version of events is supported by a number of recorded statements, which also shed further light on the motive:

• Churchill wrote: "It would be a mistake to suppose that the fate of Japan was settled by the atomic bomb. Her defeat was certain before the first bomb fell".
• US Admiral William D. Leahy, Chief of Staff to President Truman, said: "The use of this barbarous weapon at Hiroshima and Nagasaki was of no material assistance in our war against Japan. The Japanese were already defeated and ready to surrender".
• US Admiral 'Bull' Halsey in 1946 said: "The first atomic bomb was an unnecessary experiment ... It was a mistake to ever drop it ... [The scientists] had this toy, and they wanted to try it out, so they dropped it ..."
• Professor J K Galbraith, the official US investigator in Japan in 1945, said: "The bombs fell after the decision had been taken by the Japanese government to surrender."

---

* Paul Ham: *Hiroshima Nagasaki.* Harper Collins Australia (2010)

Generals Eisenhower and Arnold, and Admirals Nimitz and King also considered the atomic bombings either militarily unnecessary, morally reprehensible, or both. So why did the US drop the two bombs when surrender was on the table?

General MacArthur, however, had no compunction in his determination to test the bombs on cities with civilian populations using the presence of some military facilities as justification. In the subsequent Korean War the policy he advocated was so aggressive – including dropping over 30 nuclear bombs – that he was relieved of his command.

Several contemporary scientific accounts refer to the bombings as 'experiments' using a Uranium 235 bomb on Hiroshima, and a Plutonium 239 one on Nagasaki despite this type having been successfully tested at Alamogordo, New Mexico on 16 July 1945.

Perhaps most importantly the US Government wanted to demonstrate that they were technically ahead of the Soviets. US Secretary of War Henry Stimson later admitted that the bombs were used "to gain political advantage over the Soviet Union in the post-war situation".

In summary, the US Strategic Bombing Survey Report (July 1946) concluded "that certainly prior to 31 December 1945, and in all probability prior to 1 November 1945, Japan would have surrendered even if the atomic bombs had not been dropped, even if Russia had not entered the war, and even if no invasion had been planned or contemplated."

It was then convenient for the West to allow the myth to linger through the Cold War when we were led to believe the Soviets might attack the West with nuclear weapons. But in his book *Armageddon and Paranoia* Sir Roderic Braithwaite (UK Ambassador to the USSR from 1998-1992) unequivocally states "There is no evidence that the Russians ever hoped to incorporate Western Europe by military means". So is this yet another myth?

On this 75th anniversary of the 'experimental' attacks on Hiroshima and Nagasaki it is perhaps an appropriate time to question whether spending £200Bn on *Trident* over the next 30 years, is a good use of tax payers' money, bearing in mind that we have a massive national debt because of the pandemic, and have had no nuclear threats for at least the last 25 years ... in proof of which our *Trident* missiles have not been targeted and have been at 2 to 3 days' notice to fire since 1994.

Appendix II

International Law and Nuclear Weapons

The following is an 'aide memoire' timeline of some of the more important International Laws that apply to the use of nuclear weapons. It is not comprehensive and reference should be made to the original documents for complete understanding.

1950 The Nuremberg Principles (i.e. the Principles of International Law Recognised in the Charter of the Nuremberg Tribunal and in the Judgment of the Tribunal) are formulated by the International Law Commission. **Principle IV** states '*The fact that a person acted pursuant to order of his Government or of a superior does not relieve him from responsibility under international law, provided a moral choice was in fact possible to him.*'

2004 The Joint Services Manual of The Law of Armed Conflict (Article 1647.3) states that: '*A serviceman is under a duty not to obey a manifestly unlawful order.*' This is consistent with Article 33 of the Rome Statute of the ICC.

1949 The Geneva Conventions include provision for protection of civilians in time of war.

1 July 1968 UK signs and then ratifies (1970) The Treaty on the **Non-Proliferation of Nuclear Weapons (NPT)** by which the non-nuclear-weapon states agree never to acquire nuclear weapons and the nuclear-weapon states agree to share the benefits of peaceful nuclear technology and most importantly to pursue in good faith negotiations leading to nuclear disarmament.

12 December 1977 Additional Protocol 1 to the Geneva Conventions adds numerous provisions for the protection of civilian populations. The UK signs the Protocol on the understanding that the new rules in it do not apply to nuclear weapons (see 1998 below).

8 July 1996 The International Court of Justice Advisory Opinion

is given on a question submitted by the UN General Assembly: *'Is the threat or use of nuclear weapons in any circumstance permitted under international law ?'*

A. Unanimously,

There is in neither customary nor conventional international law any specific authorization of the threat or use of nuclear weapons.

B. By eleven votes to three,

There is in neither customary nor conventional international law any comprehensive and universal prohibition of the threat or use of nuclear weapons as such.

IN FAVOUR: President Bedjaoui (**Algeria**); Vice-President Schwebel (**US**); Judges Oda (**Japan**), Guillaume (**France**), Ranjeva (**Madagascar**), Herczegh (**Hungary**), Shi (**China**), Fleischhauer (**Germany**), Vereshchetin (**Russia**), Ferrari Bravo (**Italy**), Higgins (**UK**).

AGAINST: Judges Shahabuddeen (**Guyana**), Weeramantry (**Sri Lanka**), Koroma (**Sierra Leone**).

C. Unanimously,

A threat or use of force by means of nuclear weapons that is contrary to Article 2, paragraph 4, of the United Nations Charter and that fails to meet all the requirements of Article 51, is unlawful.

D. Unanimously,

A threat or use of nuclear weapons should also be compatible with the requirements of the international law applicable in armed conflict, particularly those of the principles and rules of international humanitarian law, as well as with specific obligations under treaties and other undertakings which expressly deal with nuclear weapons.

E. By seven votes to seven, by the President's casting vote,

It follows from the above-mentioned requirements that the threat or use of nuclear weapons would generally be contrary to the rules of international law applicable in armed conflict, and in particular the principles and rules of humanitarian law.

However, in view of the current state of international law, and of the elements of fact at its disposal, the Court cannot conclude definitively whether the threat or use of nuclear weapons would be lawful or unlawful in an extreme circumstance of self-defence, in which the very survival of a State would be at stake;

IN FAVOUR: President Bedjaoui; Judges Ranjeva, Herczegh, Shi, Fleischhauer, Vereshchetin, Ferrari Bravo.

AGAINST: Vice-President Schwebel; Judges Oda, Guillaume, Shahabuddeen, Weeramantry, Koroma, Higgins.

President's independent Declaration
'*I cannot sufficiently emphasize that the Court's inability to go beyond this statement of the situation can in no way be interpreted to mean that it is leaving the door ajar to recognition of the legality of the threat or use of nuclear weapons.*'

F. Unanimously,
There exists an obligation to pursue in good faith and bring to a conclusion negotiations leading to nuclear disarmament in all its aspects under strict and effective international control.

10 September 1996 Comprehensive Nuclear Test Ban Treaty opened for signature.

21 January 1998 Additional Protocol I to the Geneva Conventions. On ratification, the UK confirms its understanding that '*the rules introduced by the Protocol ... do not have any effect on and do not regulate or prohibit the use of nuclear weapons.*'

Late 1990s UK Government changes its policy on use of nuclear weapons from Second Strike retaliation for a nuclear strike on UK/NATO to one of deliberate ambiguity in which nothing is defined and so could include First Use against a non-nuclear threat or attack outside of UK/NATO. References to this revised policy include:

• **20 March 2002** The UK Defence Secretary, Geoffrey Hoon, in an interview with the BBC, says the UK is prepared to use nuclear weapons against rogue states such as Iraq if they use *"weapons of mass destruction"* i.e. not limited to nuclear weapons.

• **8 May 2015** Government White Paper states that the UK *'will not rule in or out the first use of nuclear weapons'.*

• **12 February 2018** in written response to an enquiry from Cdr R Forsyth: *'It is essential … that we don't define precisely when, how and at what scale we would contemplate employing them.'*

1 July 2002 The Rome Statute of The International Criminal Court is ratified by the UK. The Statute provides for a war crime of knowingly causing excessive incidental civilian death, injury or damage in the course of an international armed conflict, which is an offence under both domestic statute, international treaty and customary law.

22 February 2017 The UK amends its Optional Clause Declaration by which it accepts the Contentious Jurisdiction of the ICJ. The revised Declaration includes a reservation excluding from the Court's jurisdiction any cases related to nuclear disarmament and/or nuclear weapons unless the four other Nuclear Non-Proliferation Treaty (NPT) nuclear-weapon States have also accepted the Court's jurisdiction and are party to the proceedings in question.

7 July 2017 The **Treaty on the Prohibition of Nuclear Weapons (TPNW).** 122 non-nuclear member states of the UN General Assembly, frustrated by the lack of progress by the NPT Nuclear Weapon States to reduce their weapon stocks, vote to adopt this treaty. The UK does not sign the Treaty.

As of October 2020, 84 States have signed the Treaty; of which 47 have ratified or acceded out of the 50 required for it to enter into force.

Appendix III

UK Nuclear Weapons

Resolution Class (A3 Polaris missile) Submarines carried 16 missiles fitted with 3 warheads each.

- Range 2500 nautical miles
- **Each warhead** (200 Kt) was roughly equivalent to **12 x Hiroshima***
- **1 missile with 3 warheads** was therefore equivalent to **36 x Hiroshima**
- **A full 16 missile salvo** would have been equivalent to **576 x Hiroshima.**

Vanguard Class (D5 *Trident* missile) Submarines can carry 16 missiles* with up to 8 warheads each

- Range 7500 nautical miles
- **Each warhead** (100 Kt) is roughly equivalent to **6 x Hiroshima**
- **1 missile with 8 warheads** is therefore equivalent to **48 x Hiroshima**
- **A full 16 missile salvo** is equivalent to **768 x Hiroshima**

* The UK has reduced its onboard loadout of weapons. Each *Trident* submarine now carries only 8 missiles with a total of 40 warheads dispersed amongst them. So total destructive capability is much reduced at 240 x Hiroshima. Targeting data is not loaded into missiles on patrol but would be if a threat was imminent.

Dreadnought Class (D5 *Trident* missile) Submarines – this successor to the present Vanguard Class will carry 12 missiles with up to 8 warheads each
- Range 7500 nautical miles
- **Each warhead** (100 Kt) is roughly equivalent to **6 x Hiroshima** (see note below)
- **1 missile with 8 warheads** is therefore equivalent to **48 x Hiroshima**

• **A full 12 missile salvo** is equivalent to *576* **x Hiroshima**

Note: In February 2020 the UK Government, in response to an inadvertent leak by US Government officials (see Appendix V following), confirmed that the UK Government was working on a new generation warhead for Royal Navy Trident submarines as part of a joint US/UK W93 programme.

Radiation effect is far harder to assess as it is entirely dependent on blast height and wind direction/force and **could affect millions of square miles downwind.**

Appendix IV
UK Dependency on US

When the Government says UK *Trident* is 'Independent' they are being very economical with the facts. Whilst it is correct that RN missiles do not require specific US aid for targeting, launch or guidance in flight, with the notable exception of supply of missiles in the first case, the UK's deep dependency on US technical and political support means that the US does have the tools to inhibit or frustrate launch if it so wished.

- '(The *Trident* Weapon System) is ... a hostage to American goodwill ... the dependency is critical and will continue to be' (*Professor Colin Gray in evidence to the Defence Committee in 2006*)

- 'If the United States were to withdraw their cooperation completely, the UK nuclear capability would probably have a life expectancy measured in months' (*Report published by British American Security Information Council July 2104. Cross party groups of both nations comprise BASIC's members*)

The UK Parliament's Defence Select Committee detailed report of UK dependency on US support (see Appendix V) shows that the level of dependency is significantly higher than the Government would lead the public to believe. Not included in the report is the fact that the UK is designing and building (with US assistance) a common 12 missile module for both USN and RN *Trident* successor submarines. This is planned to go to sea with the RN before the USN.

Appendix V

UK Parliament Select Committee on Defence 7 March 2006 (para numbers are as in Annex B to their report)

UK's Trident System Not Truly Inependent

33. Acquiring *Trident* gave the UK a greater nuclear weapons capability than it could ever have achieved on its own. This enhanced capacity, however, had significant consequences.

34. The fact that, in theory, the British Prime Minister could give the order to fire *Trident* missiles without getting prior approval from the White House has allowed the UK to maintain the façade of being a global military power. In practice, though, it is difficult to conceive of any situation in which a Prime Minister would fire *Trident* without prior US approval. The US would see such an act as cutting across its self-declared prerogative as the world's policeman, and would almost certainly make the UK pay a high price for its presumption. The fact that the UK is completely technically dependent on the US for the maintenance of the *Trident* system means that one way the US could show its displeasure would be to cut off the technical support needed for the UK to continue to send *Trident* to sea.

35. In practice, the only way that Britain is ever likely to use *Trident* is to give legitimacy to a US nuclear attack by participating in it. There are precedents for the US using UK participation in this way for conventional military operations. The principal value of the UK's participation in the recent Iraq war was to help legitimise the US attack. Likewise the principal value of the firing of UK cruise missiles as part of the larger US cruise missile attack on Baghdad was to help legitimise the use of such weapons against urban targets.

36. The most likely scenario in which *Trident* would actually be used is that Britain would give legitimacy to a US nuclear strike by participating in it.

37. The well-established links between the US Strategic Command (STRATCOM), in Omaha Nebraska and the UK's Permanent Joint Headquarters in Northwood, London would facilitate the planning of such attacks. In a crisis the very existence of the UK *Trident* system might make it difficult for a UK prime minister to refuse a request by the US president to participate in an attack.

38. The UK *Trident* system is highly dependent, and for some purposes completely dependent, on the larger US system. The assembling of information available in the US, but kept secret in Britain, by John Ainslie in his 2005 report *The Future of the British bomb*, shows how extensive this dependency is (see table below).

39. The UK's dependency on the US has operational significance. For example, the UK's reliance on US weather data and on navigational data provided by the US Global Positioning System (GPS) means that, should the USA decide not to supply this data, the capacity of the UK's *Trident* missiles to hit targets would be degraded.

40. Conversely, the close relationship between US and UK systems also means that the upgrades to the US *Trident* system have already been incorporated into the UK *Trident* system. The Royal Navy's adoption of the new US fire control system has most likely already improved its capacity to retarget its *Trident* missiles rapidly in order to hit a range of targets outside Russia—thereby adding to other states' concerns that they could be the target of a combined US/UK *Trident* strike.

System	Degree of dependency
Warhead	The UK warhead is a copy of the US W76 warhead.
Arming, fusing and firing system	This triggers the explosion. The model used in UK warheads was designed by the US Sandia Laboratory and is almost certainly procured from the US.

High-explosive (HE)	This starts the nuclear explosion. The UK uses a different HE to the US. Key explosives calculations for the US warhead cannot simply be duplicated so US labs assess the UK HE's long-term performance.
Neutron generator	This initiates nuclear fission. The neutron generator used in UK warheads is the MC4380, which is manufactured in the US and acquired "off the shelf".
Gas reservoir	This supplies tritium to boost the fission process. It is most likely that the reservoir used in UK warheads is manufactured in the US. UK gas reservoirs are filled with tritium in the USA.
Re-entry body shell	This is the cone-shaped body which contains the warhead. The UK purchases the Mark 4 re-entry body shell from the US.
The D5 missile	The UK does not own its *Trident* missiles—they are leased from the US. UK *Trident* submarines must regularly visit the US base at King's Bay, Georgia to return their missiles to the US stockpile for maintenance and replace them with others.
Guidance system	The Mark 6 guidance system used on the UK's *Trident* D5 missiles is designed and made in the US by Charles Stark Draper Laboratories.
Submarines	UK Vanguard-class *Trident* submarines are UK-made, but many aspects of the design are copied from US submarines and many components are bought from the US.
Navigation	The high accuracy of the *Trident* D5 missile depends on the submarine's position being precisely determined. This is achieved using

two systems: GPS, which relies on satellites, and the Electrostatically Supported Giro Navigation System (ESGN), which uses gyroscopes. In both cases UK *Trident* submarines uses the same US system as the US Navy submarines. The US has the ability to deny access to GPS at any time, rendering that form of navigation and targeting useless if the UK were to launch without US approval.

Targeting	Target packages are designed and formatting tapes produced on shore, then stored on the submarine—using US software at each stage.
Onshore targeting	The software installed in the computers at the Nuclear Operations and Targeting Centre in London is based on US models and is probably derived from the US Navy's Submarine Launched Ballistic Missile Integrated Planning System.
Weather and gravity data	The US Navy supplies local gravitational information and forecasts of weather over targets, both of which are vital to high missile accuracy, to US and UK submarines.
Fire control system (FCS)	Used to assign targets to the warheads on the submarines. UK submarines carry a slightly different model to that on US submarines. However, all the hardware and software used by the system is US-produced. The hardware is produced by General Dynamics Defense Systems. The contracts show that the UK uses similar, if not quite identical, software.
Management	British nuclear warheads are designed and made at Aldermaston near Reading. Aldermaston is part managed by the US corporation Lockheed Martin. Repairs to

Britian's *Trident* submarine are carried out at Devonport, which is part managed by another US corporation, Halliburton.

Research and development

There is extensive cooperation between Aldermaston and America's nuclear weapon laboratories – Los Alamos in New Mexico and Sandia and Lawrence Livermore in California.

Testing

The W76 warhead was tested at the US nuclear test site in Nevada in the early 1990s. The UK has no test site of its own. The missiles are test launched from British submarines under US supervision at Cape Canaveral off the Florida coast. These tests are analysed by the Applied Physics Laboratory (APL) at Johns Hopkins University and by the Charles Stark Draper Laboratories.

Appendix VI

Submission by Commander R Forsyth RN (Ret'd) to the Integrated Review of Security, Defence, Development and Foreign Policy
(Submitted 10 September 2020)

1. In common with many of my peers, I am concerned about the state into which the Royal Navy has declined. This has unquestionably been caused by successive cuts in public spending. Yet it is noticeable that there is one part of the defence budget that is not only protected but continues to grow – the proportion devoted to the Continuous at Sea Deterrent (CASD). The UK's conventional war-fighting capability would seem to have been sacrificed in order to preserve its nuclear one. Some £150Bn+ will be needed over the next 30 years to maintain CASD and replace the four *Vanguard* class SSBNs with the *Dreadnought* class. This is sucking the life blood out of the Navy. Some serious questions therefore need to be asked about the requirement for, and affordability of, the deterrent; particularly in the light of the substantial national debt the UK has incurred combatting Covid-19.

2. The UK's *Trident* missiles have not been targeted and have been at 2-3 days' notice to fire since the mid-1990s. This indicates neither any nuclear threat in that period; nor, according to Sir Roderic Braithwaite (UK Ambassador to the USSR 1991-92), was there ever a Soviet intention to occupy any part of Western Europe.[1] This undermines the justification for the Western allies to plan for nuclear retaliation. It seems reasonable to assume that President Putin's nuclear posturing is just that. Rogue States such as Iran, North Korea and Syria do not pose a nuclear threat to UK/NATO and *Trident* is not an appropriate weapon with which to oppose a terrorist threat.

3. The rest of the world is turning against the dominance of the five nuclear weapon State signatories (P5) to the Treaty on the Non-Proliferation of Nuclear Weapons (NPT) because the P5 have not actively pursued the disarmament the NPT commits them to. Instead, they are modernising their nuclear weapon systems.

4. As a consequence, in 2017 122 States negotiated a Treaty on the Prohibition of Nuclear Weapons (TPNW): to date, 84 States have signed and 44 (out of the 50 required for it to enter into force) have ratified it. Although the P5 are refusing to support it, this growing overwhelming stigmatisation of nuclear weapons will have a major impact when it inevitably comes into force.

5. Furthermore, UK Government nuclear deterrence policy – described as one of 'deliberate ambiguity' – apparently encompasses first use against a non-nuclear attack on forces deployed abroad as described by the Secretary of State in 2002.[2] This would not comply with international law.

6. The UK Government's determination to sustain nuclear weapon capability has much to do with retaining its status as a P5 member and Tier 1 military power. The reality is that this requires a credible conventional military capability; and the UK clearly cannot afford both. Vice Admiral Sir Jeremy Blackham – a former Deputy Chief of Defence Staff (Capability) expressed this very clearly: "in order to be credible, nuclear deterrence must be underpinned by strong conventional deterrence ... Nuclear deterrence is not strong defence on the cheap ... 'Big bang' is not 'big defence'." [3]

Conclusion

7. *Trident* was designed for the last (Cold) war and is unusable in present or future conflicts. The *Dreadnought* programme should be cancelled and the savings re-invested to provide UK/NATO with much improved conventional and cyber capability.

8. Political reality may require a transition period to move from one national defence posture to another; in which case a two-phased process is proposed.

Phase 1

- Cancel CASD. The *Trident* weapon system is currently not targeted and is at 2-3 days' notice to fire. CASD could be restored within this period at any sign of rising tension or threat.
- Decommission *HMS Vanguard*. This submarine is effectively

out of commission anyway with unresolved refuelling problems. These two actions would also:

    o Much reduce manning requirement which is a major problem.

    o Improve quality of life for crews now on regular 120 day patrols.

• Change UK policy to be a genuinely defensive second strike (retaliatory) posture. i.e.

    o No first (pre-emptive) use in any circumstance and only to be used if UK/NATO is attacked with nuclear weapons.

    o Revoke the UK Reservation to Protocol 1 to the Geneva Conventions by which UK does not recognise that it applies to nuclear weapons.

    o Recognise the authority of the International Court of Justice on all matters relating to the use of nuclear weapons.

    o Establish the present reduced levels of *Trident* missile and warhead load-outs as a binding commitment under the NPT.

• Cancel the joint US/UK *Trident* warhead programme. The existing warhead has a 100 year design life according to its designer.[4]

• Sign and ratify the TPNW.

Phase 2 – to be completed by 2030

• Cancel *Dreadnought* 3 & 4.

• Convert *Dreadnought* 1 & 2 to conventionally armed cruise missile firing submarines (SSGNs).

• Divert the remainder of the *Dreadnought* programme budget to a next generation SSN.

• Re-introduce lower cost, highly capable, conventionally powered submarines. This will boost hull numbers, provide a much needed inshore operational capability (e.g. for the Baltic) and be good platforms for future SSN COs to gain experience on a lower cost/risk class of submarine.

9. These actions would enable the UK to become a world leader in nuclear disarmament and improve the UK's capability to defend itself and NATO against current and future real security threats.

References

1. Braithwaite, Rodric, *Armageddon & Paranoia: The Nuclear Confrontation* (Profile Books, 2017) p.355.
2. Secretary of State for Defence Rt Hon G Hoon MP in evidence to the Parliamentary Defence Select Committee, 20 March 2002.
3. V.Adm Sir Jeremy Blackham KCB MA *Deterrence is not only about Nuclear Weapons*. Canadian Naval Review. May 2017.
4. http://www.lasg.org/CMRR/Litigation/Peurifoy_Bob_1Nov2010.pdf.

Bibliography

Armageddon & Paranoia: The Nuclear Confrontation, Roderic Braithwaite (Profile Books, 2017)
Blair, Anthony Seldon (Gardners Books, 2005)
Blowing up the Budget British American Security Information Council, 2018, https://basicint.org/report-blowing-up-the-budget/
CASD 50: A view from the other side, Robert Forsyth, *The Naval Review* Vols 107/3, 107/4 & 108/1
Deterrence is not just about nuclear weapons - time for serious strategic thought, Vice Admiral Sir Jeremy Blackham KCB MA RN (Ret'd), *Canadian Naval Review*, May 2017
Ending the Nuclear Madness, General George Lee Butler (USAF Ret.), 2014. http://www.wagingpeace.org/wp-content/uploads/2014/03/wp40_butler.pdf
Legality of the Threat or Use of Nuclear Weapons, International Court of Justice, 1996, https://www.un.org/law/icjsum/9623.htm
Security without Nuclear Deterrence, Robert Green (Spokesman Books, 2018)
The Cold War: A World History, Odd Arne Westad (Basic Books, 2017)
The Doomsday Machine: Confessions of a Nuclear War Planner, Daniel Ellsberg (Bloomsbury Books, 2017)
The Prime Minister: The Office and its Holders since 1945, Peter Hennessy (St Martins Press, 2001)
The Silent Deep: The Royal Navy Submarine Service since 1945, Peter Hennessy & James Jinks (Allen Lane, 2015)
The UK's Nuclear Deterrent: what you need to know. UK Government Policy Paper, 19 February 2018, https://www.gov.uk/government/publications/uk-nuclear-deterrence-factsheet/uk-nuclear-deterrence-what-you-need-to-know
Thinking about Nuclear Weapons: Principles, Problems, Prospects, Michael Quinlan (Oxford University Press, 2009)
Trident & International Law, Edited by Rebecca Johnson & Angie Zelter (Luath Press, 2011)
Trident Commission: Concluding Report, British American Security Information Council, 1 July 2014, https://basicint.org/publications/trident-commission/2014/trident-commission-concluding-report

96

Acknowledgements

I could not have travelled on the path I have, nor been able to communicate my research and its conclusions so effectively, without the unstinting help of a group of friends and supporters.

First and foremost I must thank **Tom Unterrainer** of The Bertrand Russell Peace Foundation whose idea it was for Spokesman to publish this collection. Ever since we met in Nottingham where he hosted one of my first presentations in public, he has been exceedingly generous with his support and in arranging this publication. He has successfully achieved the difficult task of pulling my somewhat disparate writings into a coherent thread.

Rob Green has been another constant source of encouragement and an invaluable guide to sources of information compiled in the writing of his own Spokesman published book, *Security without Nuclear Deterrence*. He, as a navigator in RN Buccaneer strike jets and anti-submarine helicopters, like me had personal responsibility for the delivery of nuclear weapons. This focuses the mind on the concept of nuclear deterrence in a way no-one without that experience can ever grasp.

International Law is a complex area in which states can 'weasel word' their way into claiming compliance. Professor **Nick Grief** of Kent Law School and Doughty Street Chambers was closely involved in the World Court Project which led to the International Court of Justice's Advisory Opinion on the *Legality of the Threat or Use of Nuclear Weapons* in July 1996. It would be an understatement to say that I am extremely grateful for his freely given time and advice on the law relating to nuclear weapons. This has required much patience by him to curb my constant frustration between the Government's interpretation of the 'letter' and my wish to uphold the 'spirit' of the law.

Angie Zelter's campaigning organisation Trident Ploughshares constantly holds the Government's feet to the fire on nuclear issues by letter and in court e.g. the 2017 Public Interest Case Against Trident (PICAT), and also carries out high profile demonstrations. We each pursue our chosen path and activism is not mine. However, I recognise the fundamental right to demonstrate and so does the law. A majority of the arrests are not brought to trial; either no charges are laid or cases are dismissed or abandoned and even when brought to trial there are a significant number that lead to acquittal. She has kindly made the extensive PICAT archive available to me for researching Government responses to PICAT's piercing questions.

Mike Kiely is a former senior executive with BT with much experience of managing budgets. He approached the *Trident* question wishing to understand why this budget alone was increasing at a time when all other national budgets were being slashed. He became curious over the fact that missiles had been stood down and not targeted for some 25 years. This begged interesting questions around Continuous At Sea Deterrence, how could *Trident's* alleged 'stood down' state be verified and would re-targeting be an act of war? If so, should not Parliament be involved, as his regular lobbying of select committees suggests?

Jeremy Blackham is a distinguished Vice Admiral who last served as Deputy CinC Fleet. In retirement he was editor of *The Naval Review* and it was he who accepted my first article for publication in 2015. I very much respect his strong and publicly stated opinion that deterrence is not just a 'big bang' and that nuclear weapons, if we must have them, should be one of two 'twin pillars' – the other being strong conventional forces. He rightly questions whether the UK's are strong enough to justify its ownership of nuclear weapons and points out that they come with enormous attendant responsibilities.

About the author

Commander Forsyth joined the Navy in 1957 as a Cadet in the Britannia Royal Naval College, Dartmouth. He served initially in surface ships where his wish to experience something more exciting than peace time routine led, in 1961, to his captain placing him involuntarily on submarine training class; in hindsight a wise decision. He subsequently served, firstly, on three conventional powered submarines then as Commanding Officer of a fourth, *HMS Alliance*. His next appointment was as Executive Officer (2nd in command) of a *Polaris* nuclear missile equipped submarine, *HMS Repulse*. This led to his promotion to the rank of Commander and the position of 'Teacher' (Commanding Officer) of the qualifying course for submarine command. This course is rightly known as 'Perisher' because failure signals the end of a seaman officer's submarine career. While challenging for the students, it is even more challenging for the Teacher who is totally responsible for the next generation of submarine captains. Commander Forsyth then commanded *HMS Sceptre*, a new build nuclear powered Hunter Killer submarine designed specifically to conduct Cold War surveillance of the Soviet navy. An obligatory two years at the MoD on the naval staff followed and Commander Forsyth made the decision that, as his sea going submarine days were over, he would broaden his horizons and pursue a second career in industry which culminated as Marketing Director of Westland Group plc for his last 10 years in full-time employment. In retirement he helped create a local TV company and became an historical researcher, author and website editor. The combination of a highly successful submarine career – in which he acquired a unique insight into the challenges that military command brings – followed by an equally successful industrial career at top level, has given him a unique perspective from which to view the whole question of the UK's nuclear deterrent. The facts and opinions in this publication are the result of his several year's concentrated research.

Commander Forsyth maintains the website **www.whytrident.uk** where further materials and updates can be found.

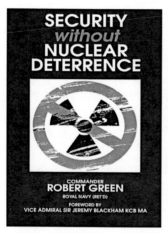

Subscribe...

Subscription rates are (for three issues): Individual subscriptions: £20, Individual subscriptions international: £25, Institutional subscriptions: UK £33 Europe £38 RoW £40.

Please send me one subscription.

Starting with Issue No. ....

I enclose payment of ....

Name

....

Address ....

....

.... Postcode ....

Email ....

Please return this form with a cheque or money order made payable to 'Bertrand Russell House'. Send to The Spokesman, 5 Churchill Park, Nottingham, England, NG4 2HF.

The Spokesman 144

WAGING PEACE
Festschrift for David Krieger

The Spokesman 145

The Spokesman 146

Payments can be made online at the following websites:
spokesmanbooks.com I spokesmanbookshop.com